A BIBLICAL
MODEL OF CHURCH
LEADERSHIP

Ducking Spears, Dancing Madly

LEWIS A. PARKS
— AND —
BRUCE C. BIRCH

ABINGDON PRESS
NASHVILLE

DUCKING SPEARS, DANCING MADLY
A BIBLICAL MODEL OF CHURCH LEADERSHIP

This book is printed on acid-free paper.

Library of Congress Cataloging-in-Publication Data

Parks, Lewis A.
  Ducking spears, dancing madly : a biblical model of church leadership / Lewis A. Parks and Bruce C. Birch.
      p. cm.
  ISBN 0-687-09285-X (alk. paper)
  1. Christian leadership—Biblical teaching. 2. Clergy—Office—Biblical teaching. I. Birch, Bruce C. II. Title.

  BS 680.L4P37 2004
  262'.1—dc22

                                                                                            2004000356

04 05 06 07 08 09 10 11 12 13—10 9 8 7 6 5 4 3 2 1

MANUFACTURED IN THE UNITED STATES OF AMERICA

For Peggy

CONTENTS

INTRODUCTION

There actually was a vision that inspired this alternative, biblical model of church leadership. It came to me in the summer of 1998 as I sat in my seminary office. The office was not yet furnished. I sat down in my one and only chair, an uncomfortably hard one with red and gold fabric in baroque pattern, which I borrowed from a repository of the seminary's furniture that had been discarded over decades, and I settled in. After thirty years in church leadership, twenty-seven as a local church pastor, and the last three as a supervisor of pastors, I had followed my call to a seminary position.

The position at Wesley was new and a lot of it was up to me to discover and define. The North Star would be this: my work must have something to do with developing church leadership. Like most church leaders I had been running too fast to capture and examine my scattered thoughts on leadership through the years. I will not say that I was running too fast to *have* them because I and most of the effective church leaders I know routinely experience the incursion of reflective thoughts, even and especially theological hesitations, in our practice of leadership. Church leaders are "reflective practitioners"; but in the dense schedule of activities that church leadership has become these days, those reflective thoughts are too often more like passing fancies than serious invitations to interpret or interrupt action. Now I was given a "time out" from the practice of church leadership, an opportunity to catch up with blurred intuitions and half-finished thoughts.

Since part of my work would involve tending to the connections between the seminary and the local church I set out on a deliberate course to read the works of the Wesley faculty. In the course of that discipline I came upon Bruce Birch's commentary on the books of Samuel, all 436 pages of it just published in volume 2 of *The New Interpreter's Bible*. During the early morning hours of that July, August, and September, before the seminary offices opened for the day, I sat in my retro chair, balancing the commentary in my lap, nursing a cup of coffee in the left hand and taking reading notes with the right. That is when the vision began to come.

For some time I have carried two strong convictions about church leadership. First, it is the most crucial factor in the reform or revival of the church today. It is not the only element, and a good church leader knows what the other elements are and how to help the congregation respond to them. But whether as its cause, its symbol, or (as is more likely the case) some mix of the two, effective church leadership is the strongest indicator of a positive fate for a congregation. Second, the way we talk about church leadership today, the language that we borrow, the sources that we quote, even the logic that we follow leaves a lot to be desired. We have grown too comfortable with a brand of church leadership that has little to do with either the church's scriptures or the church's theology. And we have not engaged the best thinking in leadership studies from other fields. It is time for students of church leadership to begin drinking the water from their own wells and, thus revived, to engage secular leadership studies with the confidence of those able to maintain their integrity in the exchange.

Church Leadership Lite

For reasons both ancient and new the church today has an insatiable appetite for the study of church leadership. A vast avalanche of books, seminars, videos, and Web sites has swept over the landscape in response to that appetite. Some of it is good and helpful, but overall much is very weak or even misleading in ways that should trouble the church leaders consuming it.

What we *need* is church leadership that drinks deeply from the well of the church's own scriptures. What we *get* is church leadership with proof texts and brazen disregard for the otherness of the Word. What we *need* is church leadership that connects with the church's best knowledge about the triune God who calls forth creation, elects a people, and directs the drama of salvation history. What we *get* is church leadership that arrogantly declares the irrelevance of such reflective work as if it were some odd Victorian scrupulosity. What we *need* is church leadership that risks a robust correlation of its scripture and theology with the very best that secular leadership studies can offer. What we *get* is church leadership that congratulates itself for dabbling in secular leadership studies twice borrowed, church leadership with a preference for simplistic formulas, catchy buzzwords, and inane parables.

The contemporary church has grown comfortable with Church Leadership Lite, with the plethora of approaches to church leadership short on biblical and theological integrity and oblivious to serious leadership study. It is time to fan the flames of a holy dissatisfaction that will send us searching for a more complete and satisfying version of church leadership.

There is too much *eisegesis* of scripture going on when we talk about church leadership today, too much "reading into a text the meaning that one wants to get out of it."[1] There are devotional exercises praising Jesus' executive abilities: how he keeps in contact with his boss (prays), how he delegates responsibility (teaches disciples), how he gives his disciples inspiring keepsakes (the Lord's Meal).[2] There are lists of leadership principles allegedly derived from the stories of Moses, Esther, or Paul—principles that upon closer inspection have little to do with these figures as presented in the canon of scripture but say a lot about some contemporary fad of self-help. More seriously, there are free-floating projections about "the church in Acts" that are used to bash the accountability structures of polity, the slow work of formation for ministry, and the everyday realities of life in a congregation.

There is a conspicuous omission of the church's theology when we talk about church leadership today. Somehow the church's history of reflection on scripture, the hard-fought doctrines of its ecumenical councils, the carefully crafted truths of its creeds, its science of God (theology), and the theological witness of its hymns and liturgy never quite make it into the discussion. The irony is that this is precisely the unique body of knowledge church leaders invest long hours and considerable money to acquire while in seminary. The double irony is that some of the same church leaders who invested long hours and considerable money to acquire a seminary education now turn around and renounce that period of formation in the name of a passion for church leadership. They have given up trying to make the connection.

There is a mimed engagement with secular leadership studies when we talk about church leadership today. We want to look like serious students of corporate culture, human resources management, and executive decision making, but we try to pull it off armed only with the thinnest books and a stash of phrases taken out of context. Church Leadership Lite offers leadership without the messiness of academic debate, leadership that soars above the mitigating circumstances of the world of business, leadership cut off from its own competitive schools and rich traditions. Church Leadership Lite carries the expression "paradigm shift"[3] into places it was never meant to go. It shamelessly exploits images like the connection between a butterfly flapping its wings in a rain forest in Brazil and a tornado moving through Texas.[4]

A Biblical Alternative

As I read through the pages of Bruce Birch's commentary on the books of Samuel an alternative, biblical model of church leadership began to materialize. The books of Samuel open in the middle of a crisis in leadership. The decline and fall of Eli's house and the transfer of Israel's leadership to Samuel is a story of the covenant of leadership broken. But it is also a very hope-filled story in that it is clear that God is the determining power in the unfolding events that begin with the providential birth of the man who will replace Eli. Samuel's strategic appearance is no accident. It speaks of a power that can bring about surprising reversals, even birth from barrenness. To a gathered people then as now there is the promise that God may be encountered in the vicinity of a leadership crisis, reacting with compassion for the people ("sheep without a shepherd") and responding with incalculable resources to provide the leader the people most need (chapter 2).

The call of Saul to public leadership is an invitation to explore dimensions of the biblical call narratives and their relevance for the contemporary church. Many persons describe a breakdown in the culture of the call in mainline churches today. A generation of church leaders is reluctant to acknowledge the encounter with the Holy Other that places all the subsequent career tests and disappointments into perspective. The gatekeepers of ministry are running scared, so determined to minimize liability and guarantee future effectiveness in ministry that they may overlook the foundational biblical call narratives. Both groups need the confirming and disconfirming information only those texts can provide (chapter 3).

Even upon called church leaders an "evil spirit from the Lord" (Samuel's name for envy) will sometimes descend. Saul's envy of David is a whirlpool of alienation that swallows Saul's good judgment first and then an ever-expanding catch of Saul's relationships. Envy is much more prevalent in ministry than is generally acknowledged. The temptations to the loss of concentration in one's own call and the providence that sustains it are multiple and complex. Church leaders need to understand why it would have been better for Saul to live out his own moment in time rather than cast envious eyes upon David (chapter 4).

There are persons apparently born to what today is called "self-differentiated leadership" and independent action, but for most persons the set-apart character of leadership is one of its greatest challenges. The story of the friendship of Jonathan and David is a rich study in the way that the call to leadership subjects our personal covenants to the strain of the larger human drama. Some contemporary writers on church leadership fast forward past the personal covenants that tear at the leader called to public service. Other writers reduce the strain of conflicting covenants by valuing the personal covenants so far above the public ones as to render the public ones essentially irrelevant. Here as elsewhere the books of Samuel hold to a realism that sometimes borders on tragic realism. You can have both—but at a cost (chapter 5). This alternative reading of the conflicting covenants of a leader is important enough to revisit in the later story of David's withdrawal upon learning of the death of his son, Absalom. The drama of private tears and public faces is intensified in this story of a parent's grief over a lost adult child. The quest for some final resolution, a grace that orders the disparate pieces of our loves, becomes even more intense (chapter 9).

Like the young David church leaders may spend their first years in ministry ducking the spears of adversaries in the congregation, of resentful colleagues, or of angry supervisors. But there will come a day when, like the grown King David, the church leader is the one holding the spear and having the power to cause harm. Church leaders have a curious ambivalence about power, simultaneously exercising it while denying it. The possibility of lapsing into destructive patterns like passive/aggressive behavior is never far removed. Church leaders must own the power they hold and the anger that arises in the course of following their call. They also must remain open to the possible visitations of an Abigail who comes along to interrupt cherished fantasies of revenge like David's intent to destroy Nabal (chapter 6).

The debate over whether good leadership is more a matter of trait or of situation continues today and has its counterpart in church leadership discussions where one or another trait theory of leadership usually has the last word. It is the witness of the books of Samuel that the secret of leadership is a robust intimacy with God. Traits and situations count, but they are not the overriding factor. David, who dances with abandon before the Lord as the ark is brought into Jerusalem, is more than the self-differentiated leader so highly prized in contemporary leadership literature. He is *abandoned to God*, leaping above the shame of institutional taboos and given over to inspirations and interruptions in ways that make him a leader after God's own heart (chapter 7).

Churches are charged environments where persons follow restless hearts, question their loyalties, and dream dreams of fulfillment. Church leaders need the same things they are there to help others find. In an atmosphere where the line between spiritual intimacy and sexual intimacy is very thin, church leaders can grow careless. They can run from their call, abuse the considerable power that accrues to their office, and initiate or allow themselves to be lured into tawdry liaisons that end in pain, disgrace, and even loss of ministerial office. Forsaking his public call and destiny, David "sends" for Bathsheba and the long story of infidelity, attempted cover-up, and confrontation by Nathan begins. But not to be missed by church leaders, or their supervisors raw from dealing with issues of litigation and liability, the long story of David's repentance and chastened restoration also begins (chapter 8).

By most contemporary accounts of leadership (secular *and* religious) leaders should ask the sort of questions that minimize uncertainty and clear a path forward to a specific destination. What traits do I need to be successful? What information must I process? What organizational culture must I penetrate? Where are the landmines? What future may I extrapolate from the present? In the books of Samuel, on the other hand, leadership is not about minimizing the presence of mystery; it is about accepting that mystery and learning to live well within it.

Although church leaders are normally consumed by action they still must harbor some final interpretation of who they are and what becomes of them in the course of their work. The books of Samuel are steeped in the subject of providence; they portray leadership as one of the social-political realities bent to the divine purpose. In the opening pages we are given Hannah's song of praise, a catalog of surprising reversals instigated by the Lord. In the closing pages we have David's song of praise to God who, against incredible odds, delivers him from his enemies, brings him out to a "spacious place," and establishes his line as a source of future blessings for many. David's worst moments come in the middle of his career when he quits waiting for God and begins to grasp, take, and subdue. And David at his best, in his early and later career, manifests a saving hesitation: "If I find favor in the eyes of the Lord." The most important and most lasting spiritual discipline of church leaders today is to grow into that saving hesitation for the sake of being available to the larger purposes of God (chapter 10).

The several disciplines for and practices of church leadership are learned by entering into a mentored relationship. Reading helps and this book argues that there are certain deficiencies in the reading of many church leaders today that must be addressed. But nothing substitutes for seeing good church leadership in action, watching its good moves from up on the wire—close enough to notice the frayed condition of the net below. Throughout my years of ministry I have been mentored well at strategic times by six pastors (Blake, Willis, Dick, Tom, Paul, and Elwood), a theologian (James), two bishops (Felton and Neil), three superintendents (Walter, Bob, and Jody), and some extraordinary lay leaders of the church (Priscilla, Conrad, Zedna, and Tom). I hope this book does honor to their importance in my life even where my conclusions show a certain cussed independence from them.

While I am grateful to Bruce Birch for his coaching in the writing process and for his generosity in offering his commentary in *The New Interpreter's Bible* series to this conversation, I want to recognize a state of affairs that precedes our friendship. Bruce is and since the days of his doctoral studies at Yale has been steeped in both the books of Samuel and the ministry of the church in such a way that he cannot separate the two worlds and is perpetually restless to discover new ways of relating the two. In the NIB commentary Bruce was simply being Bruce, and that is what made him the right conversation partner for this project. The biblical sections in each following chapter have been adapted by Bruce from his NIB commentary.

I am grateful to Rebecca Scheirer, my administrative assistant, for working so hard to make this book more reader friendly. I dedicate this book to my life companion, Peggy, who endured the tensions I try to name in chapters 5 and 9 because she too believed (at times more than I) that I had experienced the encounter I try to name in chapter 3.

Lew Parks

CHAPTER ONE

DRINKING WATER FROM OUR OWN WELLS

What Language Shall We Borrow?

There are persons in their thirties, forties, or even fifties who seem to be stuck in an identity crisis that won't go away. They keep asking, who am I? They keep wondering what they will do when they grow up. They are good workers but carry around an orphan's hunger for some clue from the past to make sense of the present and release them for an expectant future. They spend a lot of time fantasizing a career change. How much happier they would be teaching history, programming computers, or even driving a truck! And the name of these persons is *ministers*.

They have colleagues who are not quite that restless but still suffer episodes of vocational doubt. Who can blame them? If there is any truth to the scenario that society is becoming ever more secular and the church is losing its status it surely follows that ministers are losing their status, too. In the public mind they are no longer automatically grouped with the professionals of medicine and law. In their congregations they must defend their status to outspoken critics and explain their purpose to new members who come from unchurched backgrounds.

It is a time of ferment for those called to lead the church, a time of agitation that could be the yeast of new life at work or the symptom of an irreversible decline. Ministers would like to be freed up to "just do it," but find themselves delayed by fundamental questions of self-worth and social recognition. Is this work meaningful? Will it make a difference? Why do I give myself to it?

From its beginning the church has had more than one term to identify its leaders and describe their work. The New Testament witness to the earliest church's ministry comes across more like an artist's iterations than an architect's polished blueprint.

Paul's Letters, written to the earliest churches in urban centers, give us terms like *apostles, prophets, benefactors, overseers* (bishops), *deacons* (delegated messengers), and *the spiritual gift of administration.* At this early stage these terms are clearly more a description of a function than of an office. Matthew's Gospel, which comes from a time when the line between church and synagogue is becoming more pronounced, offers *the twelve, disciples, shepherds, prophets,* and *scribes.* The Gospel and Letters of John, where the church struggles to define itself against "the world" (the synagogue, false Christians, Roman society), throw into the mix terms that combine family intimacy and official status, terms like *beloved disciple* and *the elder.*

Luke and Acts, written to a church living into a mission to carry the gospel from Jerusalem "to the ends of the earth" (Acts 1:8), generates terms like *apostles, elders* as guardians of the gospel who shepherd the church, and *deacons* as charitable administrators. The Pastoral Letters paint a third generation of Christian leaders as those who exercise apostolic authority guarding faith and practice. They thrive in a creative historical moment when practices of ministry are just beginning to crystallize into the offices of the early Catholic Church: *bishops,* a subset of elders; *elders* who supervise, oversee, preach, and teach; and *deacons* who teach and administer charitable work.[1]

Two things are clear from this cornucopia of options for describing the work of ministry and the office of the minister in the New Testament. First, each generation will reinterpret church leadership for itself by accepting, adapting, or adding to the previous generation's language. The churches of the New Testament model this discipline of "being there" for the present historical moment by sustaining an active rather than passive posture in relation to the received traditions of church leadership. Even when they use the same words as their predecessors, words like *apostles, elders,* and *deacons,* they give them fresh nuances of meaning to meet the needs of the situation.

There may be more settled seasons in the church's life when the functions and titles of church leadership and the church polities which support them are everyday assumptions, but that is not where we are today. We are in a season of question and quest. Can ancient functions like *ordained to sacrament* be reframed in a way that rescues them from associations with political elitism?[2] Are ancient terms like *shepherd* irrelevant because they are so out of step with fast-paced contemporary culture?[3] Do twentieth-century substitute terms like *pastoral director* or *servant leader* faithfully capture ancient functions?[4] Can radically new ways of talking about church leadership avoid the deficiencies of traditional terms while plugging into the energy of the contemporary moment? Are we better served by immediate sounding titles like *wounded healer, political mystic, enslaved liberator,* or *practical theologian?*[5] Following the discipline modeled in the New Testament we look both to that which was handed down and to our changing circumstances of ministry as we search for a more appropriate language.

The second thing that is clear from the New Testament's diverse witness to ministry is how much of it resonates with our contemporary preoccupation with the particular ministry function of leadership. There are technical words that unfold definite leadership practices, words like *proistamenous* and its variants meaning to lead, conduct, direct, or preside (Rom. 12:8; 1 Thess. 5:12; Matt. 7:29; Acts 6:3; 1 Tim. 3:4). When Paul lists "leading" as a spiritual gift for building up the Body of Christ he specifies that it is to be used "in diligence" (Rom. 12:8).[6]

There is the word *kybernēsis* that is translated as "administration" (Acts 27:11; Rev. 18:17; 1 Cor. 12:28). In contrast to our usual ho-hum associations with the word *administration* the Greek word points to the crucial and dramatic work of the helmsman steering a ship, a job that is all the more important when the seas are stormy. When the early church viewed itself as a ship it often scripted Christ on the deck and at the helm.[7]

And there is of course the word *episkopoi* and its variants as overseers, watchers, supervisors, or bishops (1 Pet. 2:25; Acts 20:28; 1 Tim. 3:1). It is a term applied to God in the Greek translation of the Old Testament as one who watches over and directs all things. When applied to church leaders in the New Testament it lifts up the work of careful attention to the well-being of the church as a whole as well as its individual members.[8]

Along with the specific vocabulary there are glimpses of Greek and Roman models of group leadership that speak to the young church. Sometimes the models have a favorable ring as with those benefactors of synagogues that show up in the Gospels (e.g., Mark 5:22-38).[9] And sometimes (e.g., in civic assemblies, voluntary associations, households) the models serve as foils for the young church struggling to take its cues not from the world but from the eruption of God's reign in Jesus.[10]

Finally, there are case studies in leadership sprinkled throughout the New Testament. We can watch a leader striving for recognition while raising ticklish questions about the difference between power and authority (Gal. 2).[11] We can study a church leader challenging a household leader and the established codes of relationship (Philemon). We can ponder a leader who has the audacity to offer himself as a model (1 Cor. 1:1–4:13).[12] The texts that are the foundation of these case studies can and often are studied without direct regard for their application to the practice of ministry, but the opportunity for connection is available.

There are those who argue that the contemporary church's preoccupation with the subject of leadership stems from a selling out to the culture of the marketplace. They take offense at open discussions of leadership strategy and leadership power. They find conspiracy in the church's attention to its declining numbers and morale. They romanticize the church as a community that thrives without any one person overseeing its diverse energies. "What has Athens to do with Jerusalem?" And what have "purpose driven," "corporate culture," and "information management" to do with the bride of Christ redeemed by his own blood? According to the biblical witness, much!

It is true that the church is like no other institution. It has its origin in an ancient project of God to raise up a people who will be a blessing to the nations. It is uniquely anchored in the ministry of Jesus and his disciples. It is redeemed by Jesus' death on the cross and saved from historical oblivion by his resurrection. It is ignited by the Spirit's visit at Pentecost to animate and to equip persons to share good news to the ends of the earth. By God's provident interventions it journeys onward through the ages as sign and witness to God's final reign.

But the church is still an institution. It acts and feels and behaves like an institution. It has a life apart from the contributions and detractions of its individual members. It has collective memory and an evolving collective narrative. Like a family system it is a force field of scripts, codes, synergistic love, and scapegoating. Like a corporate culture it has rites of initiation, undeniable artifacts, and chains of accountability and attention. And, like virtually every human institution known to us (the exceptions are too limited to mount a counterargument), it recognizes its leaders, identifies with them emotionally, and incessantly points to them in deference, praise, or blame.

Church leadership, as a subject that provokes our critical questions and endless fascination, is here to stay. The crisis or perceived crisis of declining numbers and influence in mainline Protestant churches may be the urgent occasion for a new wave of attention to church leadership. The ever more pervasive market economy may tempt the church as never before to surrender its theological integrity for mere techniques. But neither development adequately explains why the church is and will remain absorbed by the subject of leadership. The church's hunger for a language of church leadership is ancient, recurring, and certain.

Water from Our Own Wells

Across the continent and throughout the world, week after week, tens of thousands of church leaders (ordained and lay) approach the Bible as a significant partner in the conversation of their sermon or lesson preparation. They start from and return to the immediate ministry settings in which they are immersed, but in between they open new vistas of insight through a critical reading of the scripture text as unfolded by commentaries, translations, and other tools. When the quality of that conversation is sound, the harvest is prolific. "The word of God for the people of God."

What would happen if those same church leaders engaged in a similar conversation on the subject of leadership in the church?

What if they began to drink deeply from the wells of the church's scripture and theology, not exclusively, not uncritically, but as lively sources for some new thinking on the subject of leadership in the church today? And what if they had the confidence and curiosity to test the fruits of that labor against the best in contemporary secular thinking on leadership?

This book presents an alternative, biblical model for church leadership to distinguish it from two other approaches to the subject of leadership in the church. Against those approaches that uncritically apply the varieties of no-nonsense contemporary business or management solutions to leadership issues in the church, it offers the church's book and its theological reflection on that book as serious resources for approaching those same leadership issues. And against those approaches that call themselves "biblical" but only use scripture to illustrate or sanction an agenda obviously imported from other more or less constructive sources, it offers the Bible as an active rather than passive partner in the church's reflection on leadership. As we will soon see with the books of Samuel, active partners have a way of keeping us honest and taking the dialogue to unforeseen places.

Three disciplines create and sustain the model of church leadership presented in this book. They are presented in a certain logical order, but that is not how they are experienced in everyday life. An issue of church leadership can arise in any of the fields of experience and knowledge represented in the three disciplines. For example, an article on marketing in the *Wall Street Journal* might raise questions about a congregation's hospitality, which inspire a Bible study on Matthew 25, which leads to the discovery of some helpful church history on monastic traditions. A Lenten sermon series on the relational language of Jesus in the Gospel of John might incur a wade into the deep waters of the church's theology of the Trinity, which in turn inspires new ideas for collegial leadership in the congregation. It is helpful to think in terms of a hermeneutical circle where "the partially predetermined yet open and revisable nature of human understanding"[13] regarding church leadership is played out. New energy for that circle can come from any direction.

First, the study of church leadership should exercise respect for the church's sacred scriptures. This discipline connects us with

one of the Reformation's greatest gifts to the church universal: the
recovery of scripture properly preached and taught as a mark of the
true church. The drama of an encounter is explicit. The word of the
Lord comes to us *extra nos*—from outside our prejudgments, our preferences, or the absorbing restraints of our environments. It introduces a new word from God into the situation. The word of the Lord
comes to us as our adversary *(adversarius noster)*. "It does not simply
confirm or strengthen us in what we think we are and what we wish
to be taken for. It negates our nature, which has fallen prey to illusion,"[14] because that is the only way God can shape us into the
image of Christ.

Most church leaders have been formally equipped for this
encounter. Seminary is a community for formation that places a high
value on the study of many texts of the tradition because of the value
that it places on the reading of a central text. In seminary future
church leaders learn deference to scripture through work in original
languages and the various schools of biblical criticism. They learn to
seek *the world behind the text*—its sources, forms, editing, and contribution to traditions. They become immersed in *the world of the text*
by analyzing its literary, structural, narrative, rhetorical, and canon-
ical elements. And they struggle with *the world in front of the text*
through disciplines of self-awareness: reader-response criticism, lib-
erationist criticism, feminist and womanist criticism, postcolonial
criticism, and postmodern criticism.[15]

The courteous respect for scripture acquired or sharpened in seminary becomes a lifelong discipline that informs the church leader's
preaching, teaching, and ministry practice, including the practice of
leadership. The church leader with limited time to work directly in
the original languages and schools of biblical criticism can harvest
the fruits of such disciplines with the help of commentaries like the
one engaged in this book, and other tools.

**Second, the study of church leadership should take into account
the church's theology in general and its theology of the church
(ecclesiology) in particular.** The church is an organism with a memory, a family system with a history, a corporate culture with a narrative. The church comes with nearly two millennia of experience in
self-awareness and self-description. It has argued for its fidelity to its
Founder's intentions and confessed its deviations. It has struggled to

name the "marks of the true church" and confessed its failure to live up to them. It has invited the Spirit even into its institutional life and confessed the tentativeness of its polity. It has announced its universal mission and confessed the corrupt expressions of that mission. The church has both defended the uniqueness of its clergy and argued for the priesthood of all believers. It has weighed the several scenarios for relating Christ and culture. It has pondered the reformation of its established forms.

How ironic and how unfair when those who write or talk about church leadership today choose to ignore the reserves of the church's self-awareness and self-description. They view the church as a generic institution that is without memory. Their fallback comparisons often are drawn from the world of the contemporary market economy. The doctor diagnoses and treats the patient without permitting the patient to speak. But this patient can speak! And this patient has much to offer that may disconfirm the doctor's diagnosis and treatment. The church has its own language of vitality and disease. A church leader who would lead with integrity has no choice but to learn that language and remain fluent in it.

Third, the study of church leadership should involve the courage to attempt a robust correlation of scripture and theology with the best thinking in secular leadership studies. The method of correlation is a tool used by those theologians called to a vocation of apologetics, of defending the relevance of Christian faith to the present age by showing its deep connections with currents of the present age. The best-known practitioner of the method of correlation in the twentieth century was the German-American theologian Paul Tillich (1886–1965), who correlated the gospel and culture in a format of question and answer.[16]

As Tillich studied the products of culture—its visual and literary art, its political movements, the insights of its philosophy, sociology, and psychoanalysis—he detected certain recurring "existential" questions. He viewed these questions as self-evident and universal. The method of correlation facilitates the conversation between such questions and the announced claims of the Christian gospel in a way that shows the interdependence of both without canceling the integrity of either. *Where is an ultimate concern worthy of our allegiance?* (God above gods). *Where is a knowledge that transforms per-*

sons? (revelation). *Where is the cure to estrangement?* (forgiveness). *What preserves us against the threat of nonbeing?* (eternal life and the kingdom of God).

Douglas John Hall argues for adjustments to Tillich's method of correlation to make it more compatible with contemporary experience. Tillich's "existential" questions and gospel answers are presented without contextual sensitivity. They are formulated too abstractly; they lack a place consciousness. Hall practices theology from the confessional stance of a twenty-first-century North American where the questions of existence must be formulated with historical specificity and where the Christian answers must be delivered in a post-Christian climate.[17] *How can we make absolute claims for God in the context of our immediate experience of cultural pluralism? How do we talk about God after Auschwitz? How do we speak Christian realism when the prevailing ideology in North America is political-economic optimism? How do we talk about mission in a climate of post-colonial bitterness? How do we talk about the image of God when creation is threatened by human domination and abuse?*[18]

Tillich's method of correlation invites us to consider the body of secular leadership studies as a product of the culture contributing to the existential questions that call for answers from the Christian message.[19] Why not invite into the method of correlation the creative cultural products of long-standing and responsible leadership debates over trait versus situation, power versus authority, and transactional versus transforming leadership?[20] If *Guernica*, why not chaos theory applied to organizations? If Beethoven's Fifth Symphony, why not Senge's *Fifth Discipline?* And why not anticipate that there is a relevant Christian word in response to the existential questions that arise from such encounters?

Hall's refinement of the method of correlation invites us to formulate the challenges of leadership studies with contextual specificity. In particular Hall's analysis of the North American ideology of political-economic optimism[21] offers potential ground for intense engagement. There are issues of vision and enterprise. There are debates on corporate values and worldviews. There are arresting case studies in leadership integrity and lifestyle. They beg for the voice of theological analysis and may be receptive to the act of theological reframing. But the traffic runs both ways. These issues, debates, and case studies also call church leaders back to the intractable realities of practice. They counter tendencies to misuse theology as escape.

The Books of Samuel

The decision to begin an alternative, biblical model for church leadership with 1 and 2 Samuel was accidental (see introduction), but the decision to remain there was not. There is much to be learned about church leadership by exercising respect for this particular portion of scripture, by launching forays into the church's theology from this base camp, and by practicing the method of correlation with this partner.

Leadership is a central theme in the books of Samuel. The first chapters take us right into the heart of a leadership crisis. The present regime of priests, Eli's household, is corrupt. The central religious symbol of the people, the ark, is now in enemy hands. There is what the commentary describes as a "reverse Exodus"[22] occurring. The people of God are still a mere collection of tribes diffused and passive before their external threats. Will God provide a leader, someone who will harness Israel's energies, forge a corporate identity, and point the way forward? The opening story is about the birth of that leader. Hannah's barrenness and the improbable birth of Samuel set the tone for all future talk about leadership in the books of Samuel. As in Hannah's song of deliverance, it is consistently God-centered. "The LORD will judge the ends of the earth; / he will give strength to his king, / and exalt the power of his anointed" (1 Sam. 2:10).

The decline and fall of Eli's house and the transfer of Israel's leadership to the prophet Samuel is the first of three major leadership transitions in the books of Samuel. Next comes the change from a theocracy to a monarchy as the people clamor for a king "like the other nations" and Samuel eventually anoints Saul. And after that there is the deterioration of Saul's leadership and the transfer of kingship to the house of David. There is a raw, pioneer generation seriousness about leadership issues in Samuel that makes these texts such compelling reading in times of church leadership crisis or change. And the three leadership transitions with their respective lead actors (Samuel, Saul, and David) generate scores

24

of subplots that are intriguing ports of entry for additional reflection on leadership.

Add to its prevalence this characteristic: *leadership in the books of Samuel is presented with an unyielding realism.* The voice is one of historical realism, what the commentary identifies as a "prophetic edition"[23] of the work of the Deuteronomistic historian. The prophetic criticism of institutional forms is especially pronounced in 1 Samuel 1–3 (the decline and fall of the house of Eli), 7–15 (Israel demands a king), 16 (the anointing of David), 28 (the death of Saul), 2 Samuel 7 (David's plan to build a temple), 11–12 (David commits adultery with Bathsheba), and 24 (David orders a census).

The final word at the end of 2 Samuel is basically positive: the political and economic structures—kingship, the house of David, Jerusalem, commerce, centralized government—that have arisen through and sometimes in spite of its leaders are beneficial.[24] Israel has become transformed; it is now united and capable of facing its crises as a nation-state. But the path there was neither straight nor smooth and the books of Samuel do not hesitate to name the detours and point to the bumps.

This voice of historical realism gives us leaders on their off days as well as the days they are on, shows how close even great leaders can come to throwing it all away, and reveals to us the private struggles behind the confident public faces of leaders. The books of Samuel have a special resonance for a generation that has become suspicious of institutions and fed up with professionally packaged propaganda. It is especially welcome to the hard-working pastor at the church on East Main Street who has had it with theologians, bureaucrats, and consultants who are always pointing to some Real Church "over there." Talk to us about leaders as superhumans whose success stories can be duplicated anywhere, and our eyes glaze over while our minds start to wander. Talk to us, as the books of Samuel do, about leaders tempted to envy, anger, and lust, or about leaders that have their hearts broken by grown children, and you've got our attention.

To its prevalence and realism add one more characteristic: *leadership in the books of Samuel is preserved in narrative richness.* The sheer drama of leadership, its brilliant triumphs and glaring failures, is preserved in stories that engage the mind and the heart. Stories like Samuel's call, the friendship of David and Jonathan, and the regression

of Saul have a "ring of truth" about them. One of the most significant characteristics of this stage of the telling of Israel's story is the
attention given to personality.[25] In the books of Samuel we are given
full-blown characters whose actions are both reflective and physical.
It becomes possible to see Samuel, Saul, and especially David with a
fullness we cannot see with other leaders in scripture like the patri-
archs or judges. In addition to these three main actors there are a
dozen or so in the supporting cast whose portraits are drawn with
intriguing detail: Hannah, Eli, Abigail, Nathan, Michal, Absalom,
Joab, and others.

Even those who prefer to treat leadership as a science with reliable
instruments of measure yielding quantifiable results reach a point in
their work when they must either supplement their findings by or test
them against biographies, histories, and case studies. Narrative is and
always has been an inescapable tool for the study of leadership.[26] The
stories in the books of Samuel open us to the intangible factors and
outright mysteries involved in the rise and fall of leadership. There
are questions that cannot be answered by intelligence quotients,
Meyers-Briggs type, or peer review feedback. How is it that someone
out of nowhere ("I took you from the pasture," the Lord says of
David) is elevated past more credible candidates? How can it be that
certain leaders who have everything going their way still self-
destruct? Where do some persons receive their sense of
timing or their off-the-wall inspirations that save the day? The
stories of the books of Samuel invite us to fathom leadership as the
stuff of comedy, of tragedy, and behind everything else, of providence.

To talk about leadership from a narrative of providence is to name
the most dramatic point of all: *leadership in the books of Samuel incessantly raises the question of God.* What power behind the stars
responds to social chaos by sending a leader? Who ultimately calls
leaders and coaxes them toward their futures? Who finally judges
leaders when they err and holds them to account when they repent?
From whom do leaders receive their visions for a just society and
their inspirations for compassion? How shall leaders order their
loves? Why should leaders keep marching forward when the fight
looks so hopeless?

The books of Samuel begin and end with poetry about a divine
purpose in the world. Between Hannah's song (1 Sam. 2:1-10) and

David's song (2 Sam. 22:2-51) the same claim appears in countless direct and indirect forms: the fundamental factor in all events, including the exercise of leadership, is God's presence and power.[27] Human initiative matters but is not ultimately decisive.[28] What is decisive is God the Most High who rides upon the cherub, reaches from on high, confounds enemies, and delivers the leader and God's people to "a broad place" (2 Sam. 22:20). This claim above all others from the books of Samuel offers the promise of a model of leadership that can reframe old questions, open new conversations, and inspire bold action.

CHAPTER TWO

SHEEP WITHOUT A SHEPHERD

1 Samuel 2:22–3:21
I will raise up for myself a faithful priest, who shall do according to what is in my heart and in my mind. I will build him a sure house, and he shall go in and out before my anointed one forever. (2:35)

A Crisis of Leadership

The opening pages of 1 and 2 Samuel take us into the heart of a crisis of leadership. The loose confederations of tribes that make up Israel remain the easy prey to invading armies. Eli, the leader of Israel, the priest at the Temple in Shiloh, is out of touch with his people and turns a deaf ear to their pleas for action and cries for justice. The leadership heirs of Israel, Eli's sons, have abandoned their call to public service and settled for a life of indulgence, using up their power in petty greed and promiscuous living. The situation is captured best in one of those homely details so characteristic of the books of Samuel. Eli's daughter-in-law, who would experience the leadership crisis as both a personal and social tragedy, gives birth to a son and names him "Ichabod" because it means "the glory has departed from Israel" (1 Sam. 4:21). The "glory has departed" from many congregations in the contemporary mainline Protestant church, and it is a crisis of leadership.

The symptoms of a leadership crisis are present in various situations. (1) There are aging congregations where the generation born before World War II is clearly the dominant presence. There has been a failure to connect with the baby boomers and subsequent generations, and their absence is one of the first things to strike a visitor on Sunday morning. Meanwhile the "saving remnant" struggle on, valiantly trying to maintain the facilities and staffing of their glory days. (2) There are introverted congregations that have lost evangelical confidence and no longer believe that they have something good and urgent to teach to the coming generations and to announce to those beyond their doors. To use the analysis of the church growth tradition, the little growth that does occur now is biological (a few baptisms within a congregation) or transfer of members from other congregations, but not conversion growth.[1] (3) There are congregations in denial of the pressing adaptive issues before them. They should be naming and addressing their deficit spending, or the deteriorating building falling down around them, or their failure to connect with the immediate neighborhood. But instead their energy is absorbed in "work avoidance mechanisms"[2] like petty infighting or casting about for scapegoats. (4) There are congregations where the structures of power and decision making no longer serve the mission of the congregation but instead siphon energy from it. The forms of the problem can be as mundane as a cumbersome and dated committee system or as dramatic as a long-term addiction to dysfunctional behavior. (5) There are dispirited congregations. They listen to the theologians talking about the Real Church, the bureaucrats pining for the glory days of old, and the church consultants promising elixirs of eternal youth and growth. By any of the prevailing rhetoric they are found wanting. They do not remember what it feels like to have an inner narrative and direction. They are overwhelmed by their own demeaning reflections in the eyes of unsympathetic others.

Everyone can agree on these symptoms, but not everyone agrees that a crisis of leadership is the fitting diagnosis. There are those who read the same symptoms as primarily a crisis in the church's theology whether due to the loss of a centrist Christian orthodoxy or the loss of a prophetic public voice. There are others who argue that the symptoms indicate some deficiency in the church's practices, for example, the lack of interactivity in its marketing techniques[3] or the failure to adapt to the new technology of image and immediacy. And there are a few optimists who read the symptoms as the birth pangs of a more authentic (if smaller) church reeling from its expulsion from the ranks of social and political power ("disestablishment").[4]

Each of these factors deserves the attention it is receiving in a burgeoning literature. But the curious thing about much of that literature is that it is addressed "to whom it may concern," meaning to an unspecified body of concerned lay and ordained persons inside and outside the church. Some of this evolving voice reflects a growing appreciation for the ministry of all Christians, but some of it seems curiously indifferent to the strategic role of the church leader in addressing these factors.

A case in point: for three decades the mainline Protestant church has debated and adapted or reacted to Dean M. Kelley's explanation as to "Why Conservative Churches Are Growing"[5] in the book by that title. Kelley's analysis emphasizes large, impersonal factors such as the native traits of a "strong religion" and the natural entropy of organizations. The very nature of religion favors intensity of belief and a high level of commitment. The life cycle of an institution can be measured in terms of its sense of identity and focus. The role of the leader is to be in touch with these overriding factors as he or she encounters them in the local congregation's preferred order of priorities. The leader who misreads the factors or tries to import another order of priorities is going against the grain of congregational integrity and growth.[6] There are bound to be negative repercussions.

This attitude might serve as good political advice for a pastor in the first year of a new pastorate, but it is hardly the stuff of effective leadership. It has little to say about the leader as a catalyst for constructive change. This approach overlooks the leader's contribution to the congregation's sense of vision, direction, and wholeness, and ignores the leader's irreplaceable role in helping a congregation face its adaptive issues. It has even less to say about the called and set-apart nature of church leadership, in other words, about the theological nature of church leadership. It undervalues ancient and tested church traditions about the overseeing dimension of the pastoral office. It silently passes over the biblical witness that a threat to God's chosen people is often the occasion for God's intervention in the form of calling a leader.

Listening to the Books of Samuel

The books of Samuel open in a leadership crisis that is both internal and external. Internally, the leadership at the heart of Israel's covenant faith is corrupt. Eli, the high priest at Shiloh, has grown old, and he can no longer control his sons who use their priestly office for personal gain and sexual conquest (1 Sam. 2:12-25). Externally, the Philistines are threatening conquest and extension of empire throughout the region. This crisis will culminate in military defeat, the capture of the ark, and the destruction of Shiloh (1 Sam. 4:1–7:1). Israel's national leadership is incapable of meeting the crisis.

Yet, none of this is mentioned in 1 Samuel 1:1–2:10, the opening episode of the books of Samuel. Instead, we read the story of a woman named Hannah who is loved by her husband, but childless in a world where others ridicule her as incomplete because of her barrenness (1:1-8). In her distress she trusts her crisis in faith to God, and is ironically blessed in this by the ineffectual priest, Eli. God hears her prayer, and she gives birth to Samuel. Samuel is dedicated to the service of the Lord, and through him God will transform Israel. Hannah's song (2:1-10), similar in language and theme to Mary's Magnificat, suggests the reversals of power that will come to pass through the leadership of God's anointed one.

Hannah's story reminds us that the barrenness of leadership in national life and in religious institutions is reflected in the despair of ordinary citizens and people in the pews. The story also reminds us that faith in God's providential power to transform the crisis is the foundation for meaningful change and the source from which true leadership of God's people can arise. The books of Samuel provide ample testimony to the potential for leadership that can be found in gifted personalities. Samuel, Saul, David, and an entire cast of vivid role players attest to this aspect of leadership. On the other hand, no reading of 1 and 2 Samuel can doubt that history has provided an opportune moment for transformation in Israel. The situation demands change or oblivion. Yet, in all the crucial moments of the story—from Hannah's womb, to Samuel's prophecy, to Saul's anointing and rejection, to David's anointing and confirmation—the books of Samuel make clear that it is God's providence that makes the difference. God calls the persons and works through the situations, and God does this whether persons are faithful or unfaithful.

Samuel, who will grow to become God's prophet, is the first crucial personality in the story, and he comes to maturity just as the ark is captured and Israel is plunged into crisis (see 1 Sam. 7). But, first he is born as a response to faithful prayer, nurtured by a mother of profound faith, raised in the very institution that needs transformation, and trained for the task ahead of him (1 Sam. 3). Leadership that can transform churches must begin in simple acts of faithfulness by ordinary persons whose potential is often seen by God before others notice it. This is a theme we will return to in the next chapter. The point here is that leadership crises are met first by simple acts of faith and not by sweeping programs of change. If the sheep are to have an adequate shepherd, the task will begin with what God is doing among the sheep and not with the shepherd's standing in the guild of shepherds.

Not many sermons are preached on the corruption and judgment of Eli and his sons (2:11-36). To preach this text is to acknowledge that the moral choices faced by leaders in God's community do have something to do with life and death. Relationship to God and leadership in God's name is demanding and dangerous. Those who would serve God place themselves under both God's grace and God's judgment. This would certainly alter concepts of ordained ministry in an age where too many see the role of pastor or priest as only a job or a profession. This is no less true for the roles of lay or diaconal leadership. Perhaps this episode concerning Eli's sons can help us reflect on the risky business of leadership in God's community. To treat leadership roles in self-serving ways is to treat God with contempt, and there might be more at stake than just a job.

The well-known story of the call of Samuel (3:1–4:1a) is best known to us as an often romanticized tale of the religious awakening of a young boy. Although this is an element of the story, the larger theme is the crisis in leadership of God's people. The story moves from the situation in verse 1 ("The word of the LORD was rare

in those days.") to the changed situation in verses 21 and 4:1*a* ("The
LORD revealed himself to Samuel at Shiloh by the word of the LORD.
And the word of Samuel came to all Israel."). God has raised up a
prophet (3:20).

This story is filled with elements to reflect upon as we contem-
plate leadership raised up by God for the crises of our own time.

Samuel's famous experience in the night is not an end in itself,
not a mountaintop spiritual experience. The voice of God, finally
recognized, gives Samuel a harsh message of judgment to bring to
Eli. The need for leadership does not come in generalized circumstances on the road to personal religious maturity. God calls Samuel
to a task in the context of spiritual desolation, religious corruption,
political danger, and social upheaval. The challenges of church leadership in our time are no less far-reaching.

This story reminds us that if we desire to find God's presence in
new beginnings it will necessarily require the discernment to see
God's presence in the endings of our lives and churches. We cannot
mourn so deeply what seems to be passing that we miss the signs of
what God is bringing to birth. Eli, though judged for the failure with
his sons, has nevertheless nurtured Samuel for the crucial days
ahead. Indeed, it is Eli who, out of longer experience and accumulated wisdom, first discerns the divine presence in Samuel's experience and enables him to respond. Although Eli is complicit in what
must be judged and pass away, he plays a role in the emergence of
the new. Further, his calm acceptance of Samuel's harsh word from
the Lord is a model of faithful recognition of complicity in an order
that must pass on to make room for God's new thing.

This story moves from the rarity of God's word in the land to the
ongoing speaking of God's word through the prophet Samuel.
Leadership is the human agency God has chosen to use in mediating the word of God to the people of God. God's word came to Eli
and his sons as judgment but clearly, at the end of chapter 3,
Samuel's role as prophet is the hopeful role of speaking as witness to
Israel of God's presence in what is unfolding as a time of troubled
transition. In the next chapters, the Philistines defeat Israel and capture the ark. God has raised up a prophet to ensure the speaking of
God's word in harsh times. The text, however, warns us not to confuse the word of God and the word of the prophet. The Lord

"revealed himself to Samuel at Shiloh by the word of the LORD. And the word of Samuel came to all Israel" (3:21–4:1a). We are reminded that humility is an appropriate posture for leadership that responds to the call to mediate on God's word. Our words rest on faithful discernment of God's word, but they will never be identical to God's word.

In 1 Samuel 4 Israel is defeated by the Philistines and the ark is captured. In the course of this battle Eli's sons, Hophni and Phinehas, are killed, and Eli himself falls over dead at the news of the capture of the ark (4:17-18). The wife of Phinehas gives birth to a son soon thereafter, and she names him Ichabod, taken to mean "the glory has departed from Israel." In that moment, for many in Israel, all that gave meaning to the faith community seemed to have died. But, we know because of Hannah and Samuel that God is working to bring transformation and a new future to Israel. Times of transition and renewal require leadership that can see the larger picture of what God is doing. In such times it is an act of leadership to recognize that the sheep have been left without a true shepherd. Leadership may itself supply the missing shepherd or may, as we will see with Samuel, help to raise up new shepherds and nourish them for the task ahead.

Arrested in a Season of Reluctance

The decline and fall of Eli's house and the transfer of Israel's leadership to Samuel is a story of the covenant of leadership broken. There are several expressions of that broken covenant, from leadership's abuse of power to its isolation from the people, but none quite as telling as the broken connection between God and the people. "The word of the LORD was rare in those days; visions were not widespread" (1 Sam. 3:1). The leadership that should be the instrument by which the people of God hear God, remember their destiny, and strive to live it out has become instead an obstruction.

First and Second Samuel open with a claim that the appropriate frame of interpretation to hang around certain behaviors and developments is a crisis in leadership. It is a straightforward claim, one that seems self-evident. When you see this and this and that, you have a crisis of leadership on your hands. But this reading of the facts is by no means self-evident in large circles of the contemporary church.

In many churches today, especially those of denominations that had their birth in Europe, there is a noticeable chilling in the climate of receptivity to leadership. There are alternative narratives of respect for the pastoral office available elsewhere[7] as well as in their own histories, but in these churches leaders encounter resistance to their initiatives. It runs all the way from a peevish questioning of their routine behavior to the resort to secular litigation to challenge their decisions. In these churches fundamental elements of leadership have become debatable issues: its prominence, its code of confidentiality, its ability to translate social capital into action, and its use of a collective voice.

Stories like the following are becoming all too common. A certain pastor tries to get a congregation to recognize the pressing issue of its loss of connection with the immediate neighborhood. She is encouraged to concentrate on preaching and visits, and leave the business of the church to others. When she tries to introduce demographic statistics in support of a new evangelism effort, she is warned against imposing "another of those top-down conference programs that never work." When she tries to model contact in a door-to-door canvass of the neighborhood the congregation abstains with yawning indifference. "The pastor is doing her own thing again." And when she brings the parable of the good Samaritan a little too close to home in a sermon, she is criticized for being heavy-handed and authoritarian in the pulpit. She eventually gives up. She quietly decides to pay the rent in pastoral care, invest her best energies in a doctor of ministry program, and hope for a move to a church that is serious about mission. Meanwhile the dissonance between the congregation and its neighborhood approaches the point of no return.

In many churches the unspoken covenant between the leader and the led has come undone, and both sides seem paralyzed by the terms of the separation. It is as if the church has become arrested in a season of reluctance. The origins of that reluctance are not that hard to locate. Some of it comes from painful experiences of disillusionment. Clergy scandals involving money, sex, or power have repercussions that reach far beyond the immediate circle of perpetrator and victim. One of the most important elements affected is the delicate social environment of a congregation's trust in pastoral leadership. It is an environment that takes years to evolve. Once established it shows remarkable resilience, outlasting rookie mistakes, off-day blunders, and midlife distractions. But when that environment of trust is assaulted too forcefully it loses its viability and succumbs. It is replaced by a wasteland of suspicion.

A renowned church leader falls with a descent well chronicled in the media. An entrepreneurial pastor with unchecked grandiose visions leads a congregation into impossible debt. An avaricious pastor is discovered bilking homebound parishioners out of their life savings. Each such revelation alone, and certainly the accumulation of two or three of them together, can destroy the trust factor upon which leadership in the church is founded. The generous optimism of the social contract is replaced by the calculating pessimism of autonomy: fool me once, shame on you; fool me twice, shame on me.

But there is something else going on in the contemporary church that is harder to name. It is distinct from the disillusionment that follows concrete acts of church leaders betraying their call, although it is quick to cite such acts in support of its argument. *It is a collective prejudice against the office of leadership and the person of the leader in the church.* The start of this prejudice might be "the recurring populist impulse in American Christianity,"[8] with its waves of mistrust of institutions, hierarchies, and an educated clergy. But the prejudice goes deeper than the populist impulse. It has an element of malice in it that can twist truths that would animate churches into lies that disable them.

There is a way of talking about the ministry of all Christians that begins in responsible theology but ends in irresponsible clergy bashing. There are conversations where the protest against "hierarchy" in relation to leadership has become a thoughtless slogan completely cut off from the realities of anthropological, sociological, and historical existence—and therefore all the less likely ever to be able to engage them critically.[9] There are experiences of disillusionment over leaders nursed to the point that they preclude the possibility of some new creative synthesis of a strong leader and a healthy people. There is a posture of indifference to the indelible stamp of ordination[10] that leaves pastors looking like hungry orphans desperately searching the eyes of strangers for clues to self-identity, while the people of God look to far off bureaucrats or consultants for answers.

The collective prejudice against the office of leadership and the person of the leader in the church can only be described as a spiritual sickness on the corporate level. It is time to name this debilitating sickness, to unmask its disguises, and to seek remedies for the condition.

One therapy would be to look beyond the church to secular leadership studies where the debate over "the fiction of leadership" has been conducted at a reflective level for decades. The majority position in leadership studies of the past has had a tendency to romanticize the contribution of the individual, the Great Person theory of leadership (see chapter 7). But there were always others who argued its opposite, that the very concept of a single person in front of a group, conspicuously determining its direction and bearing major responsibility for its actions, is a misleading fiction.

The trade name given to persons in this second group is the Situationists because they argue that the effectiveness of a leader has more to do with forces outside the leader than with the leader's inborn or acquired traits. There are degrees of Situationists as measured by the amount of individual initiative they allow. Some Situationists only want to call attention to the importance of timing in a given leader's rise to prominence. Other Situationists point to the extraordinary degree to which certain persons inhabit the spirit of their times, living out its questions and expectations, its anxieties and contradictions. The modern discipline of psychohistory is a venue for this argument. A third and more radical line of Situationists brazenly reverse the traditional roles of leader and led. They focus on the priority of large, impersonal forces like universal history (Hegel), economic determinism (Marx), and evolution (Spencer) or, more recently, on the bureaucratic structures that penetrate every corner of modern existence (Meindl and Ehrlich).[11] No individual can significantly alter the flow of such currents, but the currents themselves will select and use any number of individuals as figureheads.

There have been few serious attempts to offer a strictly Situationist interpretation of leadership in the mainstream of secular leadership studies for decades. But the Situationist perspective has tempered the practice of overemphasis on the traits of a leader, as seen in the Great Person theory of leadership. The prevailing consensus today is that some combination of individual strength and receptivity of the organization best explains the leadership act. When someone like Warren Bennis talks about an "unconscious conspiracy" against leadership he is naming both issues of individual preparation and issues of corporate receptivity.[12]

That makes the prevailing consensus of secular leadership studies much more compatible with a careful reading of Scripture. Both would counter the exaggeration of the Great Person theory of leadership and the cynicism of the Situationist theory. Throughout the Bible, but with acuteness in 1 and 2 Samuel, God orchestrates a movement on two fronts.[13] God is deeply engaged in the biography of the individual leader; at the same time God is deeply engaged in creating a climate of receptivity for that leader among the people of God. The pouring out of the Spirit for leadership is a double cup of blessing.

Somewhere Off Stage

As God stirs a yearning in the collective heart of the people for leadership, God quietly calls and prepares the right leader for the right moment. In 1 and 2 Samuel the very public story of a crisis in leadership begins with a very private story of a young woman's distress. Hannah prays with abandon for a child and is delivered. Her song, like Mary's song after her, is filled with delight in the Holy One who "raises up the poor from the dust" (2:8). Her surrender of her son Samuel to the house of the Lord at Shiloh ("I have lent him to the LORD" [1:28]) is a profound act of thanksgiving. It will link her personal deliverance to the larger public story of Israel's crisis of leadership forever.

Somewhere off stage from the public arena a teenager submits to God's call to preach even though it irritates an unbelieving parent and flies in the face of the teenager's introverted nature and mediocre performance in school. Somewhere else off stage from the public arena God calls to church leadership a forty-something woman. She senses the connections of her life going on but in a different key that allows her more space. She feels a growing restlessness to step out for once and assume a more direct lead in the church and in the community. It would be so unlike her. Deferring to another has become a finely honed discipline of four decades. But the God who calls surely knows all that.

The teenager and the forty-something woman have years to go before they will slip into even a modest mantle of church leadership. There is more discerning to be done. There are mentors to travel beside. There are theologies to be learned and texts to be entered. And always, always there is one more test to pass before receiving recognition from a painfully cautious contemporary church. But if they do not give up, one day they will be available for church leadership. And one day the stage will be set for them.

It is the witness of the books of Samuel that God may be encountered in the vicinity of a leadership crisis, reacting with compassion for the people because they are like "sheep without a shepherd" and responding out of God's own limitless resources. God hears the pain of social chaos. God spreads rumors of holy dissatisfaction with tribal loyalties and parochial obsessions. God plants the hunger for self-transcending habits of the heart. And when God's complex preparatory work has come to fruition in both the personal and public arenas, the cue is given. Those who were called may enter stage right. The drama of a leader and a people may begin.

CHAPTER THREE

CALLED

1 Samuel 9:1–10:11; 16:1-13
But the LORD said to Samuel, "Do not look on his appear-ance or on the height of his stature, because I have rejected him; for the LORD does not see as mortals see; they look on the outward appearance, but the LORD looks on the heart." (16:7)

The Dream of a Perfect Discernment

Gatekeepers have dreams too! That includes those who keep the gates for ministry, those responsible for admitting or keeping out persons who believe they are called to exercise church leadership. In some church polities the gatekeepers are laypersons of the congregation; in others they are clergy of the synod or presbytery; and in still others they are some combination of lay and clergy. The dream is the same: they will view these anxious can-didates for ministry who come before them claiming a call from God and the gifts to carry it out not as mortals see, "but as the Lord sees."

Like many respectable dreams it is born in the frustrations of reality. No one who has experienced firsthand the sharp disap-pointment of a church leader transgressing boundaries, breaking commitments, or raising mayhem with the soul of a congregation will blame the gatekeepers for clinging to such a dream. No one who has suffered the dull pain of ineffective church leadership, the lack of vision and direction, the procrastination, the avoidance of festering issues, or the carelessness with holy things will dismiss the passion of that dream.

If only gatekeepers could see as God sees, with eyes that penetrate the most hidden corners of time and space. If only they could hear as God hears, with ears that break every code, every silence. If only the gatekeepers possessed some omniscient instrument, some new and infallible test that would pick up what is missed by the usual battery of assessment tools.[1] Candidates for ministry would read the questions and darken the circles for the answers they choose with a number two pencil. A machine would score the black dots and soon the gatekeepers would know that "we've got a winner here" or "this one could be trouble." If the science of genetics can promise a map of a person's DNA that can be read to detect future health risks, why can't the science of church leadership promise a more accurate map with which to forecast a candidate's capacity for effective leadership of God's people?

Maybe the gatekeepers will find the tool for which they are looking in the secular science of leadership with its never-ending quest to find the perfect tool for the perfect discernment of future leaders. Perhaps among the projective tests, the simulations, the writing tests, the supervisor and peer reviews, the fool-proof reference forms, and the ever more sophisticated measurements of character and performance lies the one crucial instrument the church has overlooked.[2]

The gatekeeper dream of a perfect discernment is an exercise in responsible stewardship, an honest attempt to protect the people of God from poor or toxic leadership. But like all our dreams and all our plans it must be subject to an honest reading of the Scriptures. Call stories like those of Samuel, Saul, and David may feed the gatekeepers' determination to try harder and longer to ferret out of the candidacy process persons who are destined to self-destruct as leaders of God's people. But there is also the possibility that those call stories will challenge some basic assumptions and techniques dear to the gatekeepers. They may coax gatekeepers into a worldview of surprise and paradox, a worldview that calls into question the exactness of their psychology and the appropriateness of their social engineering. The call stories in the books of Samuel, with their drama in discrete movements,[3] may confront gatekeepers with hard questions about the sovereignty of God's ways and the limits of human knowledge. In the end gatekeepers may find they have less control of the process but more hope for the outcome.

Listening to the Books of Samuel

When we turn to scripture for insights into the leadership of God's people no theme could be more centrally important than that of God's call. God calls persons to give leadership at crucial moments in the life of God's people and to join in the work of God's grace in the world. These are the stories of men and women whose lives are redirected by the experience of God's call to give leadership, and these stories are scattered through the whole of the biblical story. Divine agency is consistently linked to human agency in a partnership of salvation and grace, judgment and redemption.

In 1 Samuel there are two stories in particular that focus on God's call and the raising up of leaders for God's people in crucial circumstances. They are the stories of Saul and David and their call to become the first kings over Israel. Their calls from God, mediated by the prophet Samuel, are both alike and different in important ways. From these two stories we may learn something of what it means to discern, receive, mediate, and enable God's call to leadership in the church in our own time.

1. The most obvious point to be drawn from the call stories of Saul (1 Sam. 9:1–10:11) and David (16:1-13) is that God uses unexpected persons and works through surprising circumstances. This is, of course, a common biblical theme, seen in the stories of Abraham and Sarah, Hagar, Joseph, Moses, Gideon, Ruth, Esther, Mary, Peter, and Paul. That this theme is so common in the Bible should not lead us to the conclusion that it is trite, but that it is centrally important. Over and again the biblical story tells us that men and women who become crucial to God's purposes would have been overlooked if measured only by the usual human standards. God looked beyond these standards and saw new possibilities. God saw in Saul the "different person" (10:6) and the "other heart" (10:9) that lay within the inexperienced young man. God directs Samuel to enlist David, an eighth son of Jesse and but a boy, "for the LORD does not see as mortals see; they look on the outward appearance, but the LORD looks on the heart" (16:7). It would seem that these stories might urge the church to reconsider the standards of discernment that usually prevail in identifying and nurturing leadership in the church. It is often easier to tick off lists of qualifications than to discern the

capacity to be transformed by God's Spirit and to become one of those who manifests the heart received from God.

Saul is not just a surprising choice, but the circumstances of his anointing are unlikely as well. It is common to refer to this story as one in which Saul went looking for lost donkeys but found a kingdom. There is a word here both for those who experience God's call (like Saul) and those who might be God's agents in mediating God's call (like Samuel). The person God needs and the occasion for claiming that person to God's purposes may present themselves in the most ordinary and unexpected circumstances. The church is prone to develop "leadership training events" or "Christian vocation conferences" and the like in its formal efforts to develop and nurture leadership for the faith community. These have their place, but Saul's story suggests that a part of our energies must be devoted to listening for God's voice to say, "Here is the one" (9:17, authors' paraphrase). This will not always come through our formal programs.

Likewise, with David (16:1-13) we have a story that reminds us of the unlikely vessels of God's grace. God's choice is David, a shepherd from Bethlehem, an eighth son from a family that has no obvious pedigree. The theme of David as an unlikely instrument for Israel's hope continues throughout the story of his early years. We are always led to wonder if this man David truly is the one for whom God has prepared us, of whom Hannah sang in hope. Can this boy defeat the Philistine champion? Can this upstart warrior escape the wrath of Saul? Can this fugitive outlaw become a king? Can a man who hires out to the Philistines win Israel's heart?

It is one of the most basic themes of the entire biblical message: God finds possibilities for grace in the most unexpected places and through the most unlikely persons. To choose the youngest son, who labors as a shepherd, to be Israel's future king is to ignore the usual arrangements for power and influence in the ancient world. Unlike Saul's father Kish, David's father Jesse is not described as "a man of wealth" (9:1, the word can also mean "power"). The family tree of David is not distinguished. Jesse's grandmother was Ruth, an immigrant Moabite woman (Ruth 4:17). His grandfather was Boaz, whose ancestors included a Canaanite woman who was almost executed for adultery (Tamar, Gen. 38) and a Canaanite prostitute from Jericho

(Rahab, Josh. 2). In the world's usual power arrangements this would not be the stuff of royal lineage, but in God's plans sometimes "the last shall be first" (Matt. 19:30; 20:16; Mark 10:31; Luke 13:30), even an eighth son tending the sheep. Of course, the unlikely journey of God's grace through the line of David leads to Jesus, born in a stable, a Galilean, a carpenter's son, and a crucified criminal. But Jesus is the true anointed one (the Messiah) in whom God meets us for the most unlikely of all moments of grace. And the genealogy of Jesus in chapter 1 of Matthew includes younger sons like Jacob, David, and Solomon, and those unlikely mothers Tamar, Rahab, and Ruth.

We must be careful not to romanticize this theme. Saul and David were not persons lacking in genuine gifts who were miraculously transformed into kings. We cannot expect a sense of God's calling and authorization to give potential leaders gifts and talents they never had before. We can, however, expect that through the power of God's Spirit they can become persons that they never were before. The gifts they possess can be put to new purpose and given new focus by God's giving of "another heart" (10:9) or by God's seeing beyond appearances and into the heart (16:7). Through God's calling and God's Spirit Saul and David have been given new possibilities for their lives, and the text suggests such new possibilities for Israel as well. To read these texts in the church is to expect transformation and change if we are open to God's calling. We cannot settle for business as usual. We cannot settle for more efficient leadership. We cannot settle for success defined as safety and stability. The spectacle of Saul seized by the spirit is unsettling and disturbing. The sight of the boy David going out to meet Goliath does not match the image of the champion Israel had hoped to recruit. But "there is a new creation: everything old has passed away; see, everything has become new!" (2 Cor. 5:17).

2. Saul's call story in 1 Samuel 9:1–10:11 is shaped by a classic call narrative form that can be seen in many other call stories in the Old Testament such as those of Moses, Gideon, Isaiah, and Ezekiel. (David's call is narrated differently in 1 Samuel 16.) The elements of this call narrative unfold a theology of God's call that can inform and energize the church's practices surrounding God's call to leadership today.

The elements of this formal call structure in Saul's story are: (1) divine confrontation, (2) introductory word, (3) objection, (4) commission, (5) sign, and (6) reassurance. Most of the other call stories reflecting this structure are direct encounters between God and the called leader (for example, Moses and the burning bush, Exodus 3). In Saul's case, however, God's call is mediated by God's prophet Samuel. This may make Saul's story of particular interest to those who work in the church with judicatory or congregational groups given the task of discerning God's call in potential leaders.

1. Divine Confrontation

It is God who takes the initiative. God's message to Samuel in 9:17 concludes "Here is the man." It becomes clear that God is already at work in the events moving Saul toward his vocation as God's anointed one. Saul does not yet know this. God has spoken to an established leader in Israel to alert him to possibilities for leadership in a young man who has not yet heard God's call in his life. Like Moses, some persons will hear God's call in a more direct encounter with God, perhaps a revelatory moment or process of prayerful discernment. But for Saul, another leader, Samuel, will be first to suggest that God might claim Saul's life. In the days when many denominations had an oversupply of pastors many became complacent and were content to examine and ordain only those who somehow made their own way to seminaries and denominational processes. Saul's story suggests that leaders in the church should listen for God's voice to indicate "This is the one." We should be seeking God's guidance in discerning those with gifts for leadership and in helping mediate God's call to such persons. Our presupposition should be that God is raising up leaders, both clergy and lay. Our task is to identify those who show evidence of gifts for leadership and help call attention to God's potential call for the use of those gifts.

2. Introductory Word

This element in the structure of Saul's story sets the basis for his commissioning later. God reveals to Samuel (9:15-17) that Saul is sent to help save God's people from their enemies. God has heard their outcry, as once before when God's people were in bondage in Egypt. In these verses, the key verbs for understanding Saul's call are "send" and "save." The leader God raises up in Saul is "sent." Processes for training, evaluating, and confirming persons for leadership in the church do not themselves create leaders. They enable and equip those God has raised up and sent to the church. Such processes need to be exercised in humility as we seek to discern what God may already be doing in persons with potential for leadership. We should seek to enhance, build upon, and utilize the unique gifts God is claiming from each person, particularly avoiding the notion of some single mold from which all leaders should be shaped. Eventually all those whom God "sends" are for the purposes of partnership with God in the work of "saving." God's salvation takes different forms in different contexts and for that reason requires persons with varied gifts.

3. Objection

Saul objects that he is unworthy; he is from the least of the tribes and the humblest of families (9:21). He joins a great host of biblical objectors. Moses cannot speak well; Gideon is from the most obscure tribe; Isaiah is a man of unclean lips; Jeremiah is only a youth; Ezekiel has no words. Such objections are surely indicators that the one called has grasped the magnitude of the relationship to God, the caller. Yet, such expressions by candidates for church leadership are often taken as lack of self-confidence, failure of commitment, or unwillingness to focus. Humility in those seeking ordination is often not highly valued as a virtue by ordaining bodies. The biblical witness is clear: the call is often experienced as an intrusion, a struggle, the beginning of an uncertain journey. The church needs to cultivate a process that acknowledges these elements and supports those called in their uncertainties and struggles.

4. Commission

Saul's commission (10:1) reflects the nature of the task of salvation revealed to Samuel the previous day. But here Samuel declares to Saul that this is "the word of God" (9:27), and the prophet anoints him, a ceremony used for kings and priests. God's call to a person must receive affirmation by those who are established leaders of God's community. Samuel recognizes Saul's calling as vocation, an audacious partnership in the saving work of God. Leadership in the church, whether lay or ordained, is not a taking on of church jobs or undertaking a profession. It begins in a call from God and must be confirmed by a commission to open oneself to God's Spirit for empowerment to join God's work. Established leaders of God's community not only help discern a person's call to leadership, but also that person's potential to be open to the action of God's Spirit in leadership. Can that person forfeit personal agendas or institutional ambitions? Sadly, Saul could not and was rejected by God from leadership.

5. Sign

In Saul's story the most important sign is his reception of God's Spirit and the transformation of Saul by God's Spirit into "a different person" (10:6) with a "changed heart" (10:9). It is God's Spirit that ultimately confirms those God has called into leadership. Like Samuel, those who work to raise up and commission leaders do so in humility and recognition that we but serve what only God's Spirit can confirm. It would seem that a key element in any discernment process for those given the task of being a Samuel might be to encourage openness to God's Spirit. We need processes that do not suggest premature closure where God might be leading. We need support and encouragement for those who understand that ordination or commission to leadership is the beginning of a journey in the Spirit and not a destination. We need to model and share our own openness to become "different persons" and receive "new hearts" in our own ongoing journeys with God's Spirit.

6. Reassurance

The classic formula of reassurance is given to Saul as he begins his journey in God's Spirit, "God is with you" (10:7b). This reassurance is, of course, related to the objection. If we recognize that God's call comes often as intrusion, struggle, and uncertainty, then we, like Samuel, need to be prepared to speak the word of reassurance. The two of us authoring this book have heard years of steady testimony from many seminary students that they experienced denominational ordination processes primarily as adversarial proceedings. But they also tell of the reassurance of mentors and supporters to counterbalance this along the way. Saul was but a young man and his full potential for leadership lay ahead. He needed Samuel's word of reassurance. Likewise, David's story in his early years is filled with the constant testimony that "the LORD was with him" (e.g., 18:12, 14, 28). In a time when the church is seeking to reclaim God's claim on young adults we would do well to examine our role in voicing the reassurance needed for those called to a challenging journey.

3. The real point of these stories of Saul's and David's calling (and of our own) is to focus on the one who calls. These are stories of *God's initiative* and *God's Spirit* as the source of newness. The newness of God for Saul, for David, and for Israel does not come from calculating reason, careful political maneuvering, or discernment in recruiting. This was surely what the elders wanted and expected (1 Sam. 8). They wanted a general, an administrator, and a royal symbol of stability and safety. Instead they got Saul, seized by the power of the Spirit in ways that amazed, perhaps embarrassed, those who knew him (10:11-12). Later they got David, a boy who alienated his own king, became a fugitive, and even served Israel's enemies, the Philistines. These did not look like leaders who could manage in the people's interests. The Spirit often appears unmanageable in the world's terms. When the Spirit powerfully filled those present at Pentecost, onlookers sneered that they were drunk (Acts 2:13), and Hannah had been accused of drunkenness by Eli when she was merely occupied with God (1:14).

For the people of God, whether Israel or today's church, genuine newness comes first from *God's initiative*. The people may demand, as the elders of Israel demanded a king, but God will choose, as made evident in Saul ("Here is the man," 9:17) or David ("The LORD looks on the heart," 16:7). In the church, most denominations or traditions have elaborate structures and mechanisms for choosing leaders. It is important to examine these constantly and prayerfully to ensure that they are accountable to the choosing of God. The church's processes should always include a discernment of what God has chosen as the path to newness in the life and mission. Call is about God's leads and not the church's or the candidate's needs.

For the people of God genuine newness is not only initiated by God but empowered and made possible by *God's Spirit*. In God's Spirit Saul was made new, and that newness took surprising and amazing form as he prophesied with the prophets. In God's Spirit David calmed the troubled spirit of Saul and felled the mighty Goliath. Openness to God's Spirit in the community of faith will lead us down unexpected paths. In its institutional forms, the church is like other human institutions, preferring patterns that can be managed and controlled. When oriented to faithful purposes this can even be good stewardship. But the power of God's Spirit, constantly working to transform the church and the world, means that a central element of our life will be unmanageable and uncontrollable. God's spirit seizes, surprises, upsets, transforms, and reorients. Without openness to this empowerment of the Spirit the church cannot be made new.

The pattern of God's choosing and the Spirit's empowering is one with considerable resonance in the biblical tradition. In 1 Samuel 9:1–10:16, Saul is chosen by God, is anointed by the prophet Samuel on God's command, and receives God's Spirit. The result is to give Israel its first king. In 1 Samuel 16:1-13, David is singled out as God's choice, is anointed by Samuel, and receives God's Spirit. The result is not only a king for Israel, but also a dynasty (the house of David) descended from the man "after God's own heart." In Luke 3:21-22 (also Matt. 3:13-17 and Mark 1:9-11) Jesus is baptized (anointed) by John, the Spirit descends upon Jesus, and God's voice claims him as "beloved Son" (the language is taken from Psalm 2:7, a royal psalm, and Isaiah 42:1). The result is the beginning of the career of Jesus as Messiah, the anointed one, born of the house of David. In Acts 2 the Spirit descends and flames anoint the apostles and those assembled with them. The result is the Pentecost birth of the church.

This places us as the church today in the line of the pattern that begins with Saul. Are we still the God-chosen, spirit-filled church? Saul is eventually rejected by God through Samuel the prophet because of disobedience (1 Sam. 15), and Saul loses the Spirit. Could the church suffer the same fate? David is the "man after God's own heart" (13:14), and he is empowered by God's Spirit (16:13). But when as king he let his own desires and interests lead him into adultery and murder (2 Sam. 11), God sends a prophet with judgment to say "You are the man!" (2 Sam. 12:7). Do we continue to live out the promise of newness that the Spirit brings, or have we, like David, been diverted by our own self-interest? We must reflect on church leadership in light of the stories of Saul and David with awareness of the fate they suffered as they lost sight of God's call and began to think of leadership as management of their own self-interests. God's call is not an entrance requirement but a constant touchstone of leadership identity and focus for those who serve God's people.

Bill from Some Remote and Untamable Region

The first and last thing to be said about church leaders is that they are called by a higher power. Discerning that call and walking in its path is the first work of church leadership. Both the person called and the gatekeepers, those responsible for admitting or keeping out persons who believe they are called to exercise church leadership, live in the unstable atmosphere of divine human encounter. Both should anticipate turbulence by the very nature of the one who initiates every journey of call discernment.

Bill had been a white-collar crime detective for a federal agency in his first career, a detective who took special pleasure in "busting" offenders. His call to ministry was vivid and urgent. He left his job with its healthy salary. He sold the house into which he and his wife had put so much work. He withdrew the children from the only school they had ever known. Then he and his family trekked to a distant seminary in an obscure location because, in his words, "they get you ready to preach there without stealing your faith."

The first time Bill appeared before the gatekeepers in the early 1980s he could have been the repair technician coming to fix the photocopier in the church where the gatekeepers were meeting: navy blue pants, white shirt, narrow maroon tie, crew cut. He carried a large leather briefcase and arrived early for the appointment. Any first impressions of professionalism would vanish the minute he opened his mouth. He could barely complete two sentences without lapsing into a bravado that seemed to be a holdover from his first career. He bordered on sexism, racism, and ageism when he talked about others and on comical conceit when he talked about himself. When the gatekeepers challenged him about some tensions in the church he was serving as a student pastor, he fashioned his own little apocalyptic scenario in response. He drew sharp lines between the Righteous, who followed his latest idea, and the Unrighteous, who expressed reservation. He said he knew prophets weren't always appreciated, but whose fault was that?

There were red flags everywhere: in the reports from the seminary, in the formal assessments required for ordination, and most blatantly in the interview itself. But the gatekeepers chose to overlook them and focus instead on what, beneath the surface noise, came across as an obvious call from God. When challenged on some point of theology, Bill would absorb it like a patient who knows his own body best but is anxious to hear what the doctor says about the X rays. When corrected on some point of practice or etiquette he would assume a sheepish grin, as if his hand was caught in the cookie jar, and promise to do better next time. And he never wavered from his firm belief that he was called to lead God's people. Neither his steep learning curve nor the gatekeepers' endless questions would change that. And in the end, for whatever reasons of discernment or fatigue, the gatekeepers agreed.

Five years later Bill was back before another group of gatekeepers, and he was in trouble. He had attended a seminar on church growth in a distant city and returned to his rural congregation with a catch of great ideas. One of them was to replace the traditional worship service with a contemporary worship service. The first step was to purchase a keyboard with money the church had previously raised to repair the organ. Since the wave of the future was clearly contemporary worship, the logic seemed inescapable to Bill: redirect the money and guarantee church growth. When the administrative board didn't quite see it that way and voted down the attempt to reallocate funds, Bill was crushed.

The next Sunday morning the members of that congregation arrived to find themselves the guests at their own corporate funeral. The flowers and candles had been removed and the altar draped in black. Pictures on the walls and the hymn board were also draped in black. The bulletin heading announced the service of memorial with the birth date of the Dearly Departed given in the late 1800s and date of death as that of the administrative board meeting. As the Old Testament lesson, Psalm 90 reminded the congregation of human mortality. The New Testament lesson from Revelation 3 centered on the lukewarm church of Laodicea that was "spit out" of Jesus' mouth. The sermon was a thinly disguised replay of the administrative board meeting enhanced with apocalyptic imagery. Only the organist, now assured of getting the repairs to her treasured organ, seemed to catch the spirit of the enterprise, playing "Nearer, My God, to Thee" with a crisp and bouncy irony. Most parishioners entered the sanctuary, took a look around, read the bulletin to see what was going on, then turned on their heels and walked out. Others fled at various points in the service. Those who remained to the end stumbled out in silence. Bill left hurriedly during the last hymn without further explanation or interpretation.

The present set of gatekeepers called an emergency meeting that same week, and they were relentless with Bill. What was he thinking? What possessed him to pull such a stunt? How could he be so insensitive? Bill's thick file was opened and the chronicle of previous episodes rehearsed. Someone who served on the earlier group of gatekeepers related some hazy memories of those earlier red flags. Bill remained his own worst defense, fumbling as spin doctor for his actions and trying in vain to dismiss his detractors because of their alleged political agendas. Some of the gatekeepers twitched in restlessness; others rolled their eyes.

But Bill also touched another nerve and would not back away. "If God told you to go wake up these people, what would you do?" And that question more than anything else absorbed the gatekeepers after Bill left the room. Most of the churches in that region were in poor health. They had lost touch with persons under sixty. They were comfortable in their introversion and equally indifferent to initiatives in missions, social justice, and evangelism. They were keeping warm by the fire of a previous generation's adventure. They were getting by with biblical illiteracy and followed a Christ who apparently winked at the surrounding culture. The few pastors who tried to challenge them soon grew weary and gave in. Bill was different.

He questioned whether those other pastors, some now among the gatekeepers, had given in too soon. After considerable discussion the gatekeepers reprimanded Bill for the bluntness of his tactics and suggested to the judicatory that he needed a fresh start with good supervision.

Three years later Bill was back before yet another group of gate-keepers. This time he was in trouble for misusing his power as chair of the committee that nominates church officers. By the second year of his new pastorate Bill thought he knew who did or did not share his vision for ministry. Without bothering to call a meeting of the committee on nominations, he prepared a ballot with sweeping revisions for the annual meeting of the congregation where the elections would be held.

On the night of the meeting the conference superintendent who chaired it first learned there was a problem when the recording secretary, choking in tears, whispered hoarsely to him that according to the ballot she was being replaced by the woman for whom her husband deserted her a month ago. Did that seem right to him? It was only the first of a series of startling revelations: veterans summarily dismissed, newcomers placed in offices they had never heard of, whole committees eliminated without explanation. Chaos ensued.

An emergency meeting of the gatekeepers was called. This time there were those among the gatekeepers determined to see Bill expelled from the practice of ordained ministry. They had nearly ten years worth of clear, incontrovertible facts on their side—a trail of aggressive blunders and uncouth words.

All but two persons present agreed. One was Bill's immediate supervising pastor. He said he didn't know enough about Bill's past to separate truth from reputation, but at present he was working with Bill on some fine-tuning and they were making progress. More important, there was a core integrity and intensity in Bill's call that was forcing the supervising pastor to take a second look at some of his own compromises along the way to what many would call a successful career in ministry. "It is so easy to lose your cutting edge as a church leader," he admitted, "to become so much at home in the present corporate culture of the church that you can no longer be an agent of change." The supervising pastor recalled that even that most polished British Anglican John Wesley became convicted enough to abandon his church propriety and risk the "vile thing" of field preaching.[4]

Bill's other defender was the lay leader from one of the churches Bill served. He was retired from a career in the military where he commanded troops in the field. He said he could still read men and he knew three things about Bill. "One, he needs to think more before he talks. Two, he needs to think more before he acts. And three, he was sent by God to lead us." He said the gatekeepers already knew why the first two points were true, but they needed to understand the third. He began to paint a picture of a sleepy rural church that was in retreat. There was no sense of having good news to be shared urgently with those beyond the doors of the sanctuary. There was no attempt to address issues that consumed the community, such as teenage suicides, car fatalities, and unwanted pregnancies. The layleader said he had prayed for years that their church would be sent a pastor brave enough to stand up in the middle of this mass defection and yell, "You're going in the wrong direction, now turn around and charge!" The layleader said he had spent serious time in prayer and soul sharing with Bill and was convinced he was a man more under orders than the victim of ego. Shouldn't the gate-keepers expect some flak when the people of God finally meet up with one sent from God to take them to new places?

Once again, though by a split vote, the gatekeepers relented. Bill was reprimanded for his flagrant violation of polity. He was instructed to call a meeting of the committee on nominations and start over again. He was told to offer profuse apologies where they were due. He was advised to maintain the weekly contacts with his supervising pastor and to get some continuing education in negotiating skills. Then he was sent on his way with a prayer for new wisdom and a sigh of hope.

Behind their backs the gatekeepers were soundly criticized by lay and clergy alike who were following the story. They were called weak. They were accused of covering up. They were diagnosed as being out of touch with the local church. The gatekeepers were under no obligation to explain their decision and possibly could not have done so. Put yourself in their shoes. How do you explain an encounter with persons who believe themselves called of God and come bearing the marks of an authentic messenger? You go to the meeting thinking the agenda is *their* rough edges or maybe even the authenticity of *their* call only to find the spotlight turned on *your* accommodations and compromises. The comfort zone of *your* faith is being challenged. This Samuel, Saul, or David before you is not what you were looking for. Ready or not, you are being visited from some remote and untamable region where the ultimate meanings are.

Gatekeepers, It's About God!

Each person who comes before the gatekeepers is ultimately a mystery of human nature, a thou. When the gatekeepers face such a person they experience essentially insurmountable gaps in their prognostication. Biographical particulars are lost or forgotten, subconscious forces wait to surface, and biological factors remain undetected or are not understood. There are eccentricities of cultural contexts, changes in the meaning of meaningful, and movement in the overriding structures of history. The sum of these gaps is not an unfortunate disease needing a cure. It is a fact of existence that begs for a positive theological interpretation,[5] the kind of interpretation that is assumed in the books of Samuel where God is the power of the future that matters, and relentlessly visits persons and groups with new possibilities.

The people of Israel want a king who looks and acts like the kings of other nations. Well-intentioned gatekeepers measure by human standards. But God, who "looks at the heart," has the last word. Inconvenient as it may be, the person who stands before the gatekeepers is an unfinished product sustained in essential openness and sent by a God who self-identifies with a name shrouded in mystery, "I AM WHO I AM" (Exod. 3:14).

An encounter with one called by God is always also an encounter with God. Gatekeepers must lean close and listen intently for a voice behind the human voices of the women and men who come before them claiming a call to church leadership. If God really called this person to lead the people of God at this moment in their history, and if God has appointed this person to appear before the gatekeepers, then what message does God also have for the gatekeepers?

Is it a message of judgment? Perhaps it is time for them to surrender some of the tedious gatekeeper games of wrangling over agendas that have more to do with the vagaries of pop psychology or half-remembered theology than with the rich depths and subtle contours of the biblical call language. Perhaps it is time to receive candidates for ministry with an empirical inquisitiveness born in the acquaintance with the dialectic drama of the biblical call narratives. In the same way that every church would call itself a friendly church, every group of gatekeepers probably regards itself as biblically grounded for the work it does. What little research there is on the matter tells a different story.[6]

Is God speaking a message of grace to the gatekeepers? In sending certain persons to them, is God allowing gatekeepers a glimpse of some new direction God intends for the institutional church? That Generation X person who speaks from a radically different experience of life in a mainline church may challenge that GI or baby boomer generation gatekeeper to listen with new ears.[7] Sometimes the person who best registers the church's pressing adaptive challenge is located on the periphery and is being nudged to the center of action by God. These peripheral candidates for ministry are of an ethnic group, economic class, or culture niche not yet reached by the church. They will require some sheltering and encouragement along the way.[8] They challenge gatekeepers less at the point of conscience than at the point of imagination. What might God intend in calling such persons? Will the gatekeepers cooperate with God's preferred future for the church?

The seemingly endless parade of new persons appearing before the gatekeepers claiming a call to church leadership from God is a phenomenon of divine stewardship worth pondering. In the face of dire predictions for the church, apparently God continues to call persons to invest their lives in this institution. To use an old-fashioned image that combines mission and risk God remains in the work of enlisting recruits for church leadership. How dare gatekeepers or anyone else give up on the church now?

Because God is God, the first work of gatekeepers is to stay alert. They can never tell when the leader whom God summons for the demands of the hour will appear on their doorsteps looking like "a shepherd, an eighth son, from the village of Bethlehem, from a family that has no obvious pedigree."[9]

Called Persons, It's About God!

If the divine origin of the call to church leadership can be a nuisance to gatekeepers, it can be a torment to those called. The books of Samuel do nothing to relieve that torment! God calls with indifference to human circumstance, convenience, or timing. Human protest is a normal response, but so is the divine persistence in the face of such protest.[10] The first and last work of every leader called by God is to come to terms with the One who calls and with the demands of that call.

That brings to the fore a pressing issue of leadership integrity facing the contemporary church. Routinely persons come before the gatekeepers employing the Bible's dramatic call language to name a perceived disruption in their lives. They say they have been plucked out of a life of obscurity against all odds. They claim that a holy dissatisfaction with their present life has been ignited within them. They say there have been signs and wonders along the way to confirm. But when these persons turn to the future implications of the call they begin to hesitate and stipulate. "Just three more years until my federal pension kicks in; then I'll be ready." "My husband says we can go anywhere we're sent as long as he can drive home from his business each evening." "Isn't there a church somewhere without a parsonage that would appreciate a pastor who wants to live in his own home?" "A lawyer with a lawyer's bills can't afford too much of a cut in salary." "In five years our children will be grown, and we'll be more flexible."

The church through its gatekeepers has grown accustomed to this language of equivocation. Thirty years ago Alvin Toffler and others forecast a working world of "serial careers."[11] That world has arrived: persons are no longer fated by the vocational decisions or indecision of their twenties, thirties, forties, or even fifties. So why not answer the call to ministry farther down the road? Wasn't Abraham seventy-five when he and Sarah were called from their country and kindred? When second, third, or fourth career persons appear before the gatekeepers it is understandable that they carry more baggage then a twenty-one-year-old fresh from a liberal arts college. What else can gatekeepers do but applaud the apparent, if more complicated, work of God among them?

But gatekeepers are also stewards of the biblical language of the call. They are spokespersons for and defenders of the unequivocal character of the God revealed in stories like those in the books of Samuel. God's call in scripture is unconditional and unyielding. For every person trying to coax a more user-friendly reading of the texts there are others who accept the stringent demands of these texts at face value. There are calls from God to the young and very young which do connect. These calls preclude the politics of compromise and remind the church of its better self. There are other calls from God to more mature persons, which raise havoc with accrued loves, previous commitments, accustomed lifestyles, and rational life plans. A physician is called away from his practice, a lawyer from her promising career. A mother is called to nurture the body of Christ as well as her three small children. An owner of a five-generation family business must sell it to give undivided attention to the divine call to church leadership. Casualties of such high altitude turbulence arrive at the meeting table of the gatekeepers and the doors of the seminary all the time. They follow God's call unconditionally, and their stories are impressive.

It is ultimately God who calls persons to this struggle, not the "heavy-handedness" of some polity or the "unrealistic expectations" of some ordaining board. It is ultimately God who has placed us in an irreversible world process where there are irretrievable losses. A call to ministry that is "missed" at twenty is not happily "fixed" at fifty-five.[12] There is much good in that later call, but also much loss for the delay. It is ultimately God who draws the distinction between those who must be set aside *now* for full-time leadership in the church and those who will not but may get around to it some day. Gatekeepers do well to keep themselves from becoming triangulated in such disagreements. The argument between an unyielding God and a reluctant recruit is holy ground.

CHAPTER FOUR

ENVY

1 Samuel 18:1-30
Saul was very angry, for this saying displeased him. He said, "They have ascribed to David ten thousands, and to me they have ascribed thousands; what more can he have but the kingdom?" So Saul eyed David from that day on. (18:8-9)

In Dante's *Purgatory* the souls that succumb to envy sit huddled against the face of a cliff on the fifth terrace down. Their eyelids are sewn shut with iron threads, "like falcons newly caught, whose eyes we stitch to tame their restlessness."[1] It is an exquisitely accurate image of remedial punishment. No more sharp glances to the left or right to see if other runners in the race of life are catching up or, worse, threatening to pull ahead. No more scanning the horizon to see if someone out there has received a prize, experienced a success, or garnered recognition that, they are certain, more properly belongs to them. No more obsessing on others' gains to nurse their sense of loss or zooming in on others' losses to feed their sense of gain.

One of those souls condemned for "casting envious looks" on others is identified as Sapìa of Siena who confesses, "I always reveled in another's grief, enjoying that more than my own welfare."[2] She hated her fellow Sienese and resented her nephew Salvani's rise to power. Sapìa is notorious for taking pleasure in the defeat of the Sienese by the Florentines in the Battle of Colle in 1269.[3] Envious souls like hers carry consuming personal agendas that skew normal response to bad news and good news alike. Impulses to sympathy and solidarity are ignored. Even the basic instinct for self-preservation takes second place to seething resentment. In Sapìa the sickness is revealed in the way she reacts to a defeat. As we will soon see, in Saul the same sickness is first revealed in the way he reacts to a victory.

By the usual reckoning church leaders should be slow to envy. There is after all a certain leveling factor that comes with the call from God. God calls the young who have few resources, and God calls second career persons who must abandon the very things that once gave them distinction: rank, title, seniority, status. Both groups will humble themselves, first for graduate theological education and then for apprenticeship. Both groups anticipate careers with modest salaries and modest salary increases. They expect to live in parsonages of "official minimum standards" or to receive housing allowances that are "fair." They may even observe a dress code of sorts. If they are of one generation they wear colors that hint of monastic orders (black, gray, and brown) and conservative styles that suggest ties to the professions of law, medicine, and education. If they are of another generation the uniformity comes out in the bleached out look of jeans or cotton pants and earth-tone sport shirts.

Through the centuries, from early monastic rules to the latest edition of a denomination's code of ethics for its clergy, church leaders are called to the virtue of mutual recognition and the practice of parity in the journey of shared mission.[4] From salary and benefits to collegial respect and cooperation, church leaders are challenged to subsume personal desire for distinction to the corporate demands of a larger cause.

But even upon church leaders what 1 Samuel calls "an evil spirit from the LORD" sometimes descends. In more benign doses it might spur emulation, the way good preachers will try to outdo the great preaching of another. Or it might register in a variety of subtle behaviors that collectively we read as a "morale problem" in clergy: their poor attendance at gatherings of colleagues, the lack of support for larger programs, the distancing from leaders. But envy can become much more dangerous than that. It can rob church leaders of focus, of the ability to receive the work of ministry as a demanding but absorbing call from God with its own rewards for service faithfully rendered. And it is often the precursor to more dramatic and destructive behavior such as infidelity, crime, or subversion. First Samuel 18 offers a worst case scenario.

Listening to the Books of Samuel

First Samuel 18 is a narrative focused on leadership and relation-ships. All of the elements of institutional systems are present. There are urgent needs and crises. The Philistines still threaten the future of an infant kingdom with limited resources. There are established leaders: Saul is king—no longer the youth that Samuel anointed, but the head of a royal court with some success at nation building. Saul is also now the father of adult children, Jonathan, Merab, and Michal. There are young, talented rising leaders: Jonathan, the son and heir apparent and a distinguished warrior alongside his father (see 1 Samuel 14), and David, the young hero who killed Goliath (chapter 17) and now wins victories for his king (18:5). There are also the many other people whose responses to these leaders is cru-cial to the story.

Much of the overlapping stories of Saul and David in 1 Samuel 16–31 are episodes that chronicle the interwoven themes of David's rise and Saul's decline. What makes one leader successful and the other a failure? The testimony of these stories of David and Saul indicate that the answer can never be a simple one. Leadership is forged in complexity and the ambiguity of relationships. Even more important, the answer for people of faith lies within the complex interworking of human freedom and divine providence.

The Harp and the Spear

Before the drama of 1 Samuel 18 unfolds, we must consider briefly the beginning of the relationship between Saul and David. David is brought into Saul's service as a musician. The music of his lyre soothes Saul, who is a man troubled by an "evil spirit from the LORD" (16:14). Initially, "Saul loved [David] greatly" (16:21). But the mal-ady of the evil spirit is related to Saul's own anger, envy, and fear. A relationship that begins in love is soon destroyed. Saul threatens the future leadership embodied in David, and in the process Saul undermines his own leadership.

A famous painting by the Dutch master Rembrandt van Rijn depicts Saul and David at this time. Saul in the foreground is dressed in the turban and finery of an oriental potentate. Yet his expression is sad and melancholy, obviously that of a man in despair. At the same time he grips a spear, and something about his grasp on that weapon and the set of his jaw tells us that there is not only sadness here but also danger. There is a potential for evil dwelling in this troubled man. Almost hidden in the shadows of the background is David with harp in hand. We know the story and we know that his task is to soothe this troubled king. There is something hopeful about David's presence that provides a stark contrast to this powerful, troubled, and potentially evil man in the foreground. David is present as the future, but we know it is an endangered future. We hope he will be good at dodging spears.

Our tendency is often to define power as dangerous and potentially evil. At the beginning of the twenty-first century, distrust of those in authority is very high. In our time we have seen madness erupt and brandish the spear—in holocausts, gulags, ethnic cleansings, tribal wars of genocide, and terrorism. Even short of horrors and atrocities, we have seen those who have the power of governance or leadership as troubled and self-serving. First Samuel 18 does not absolve God of these evil spirits, and we, too, wonder why God's world should allow for such possibilities.

The narrative of David's introduction to Saul's court and the painting by Rembrandt remind us that there are alternatives to troubled leadership. Both spear and harp may represent power used faithfully for God's purposes. In this episode David holds a harp in his hand. David will, in future episodes, also be a warrior and wield the spear for good. But, against the evil spirits that trouble Saul, David comes first as a singer of hope. It may well be that the church, like David, will be called to sing in the face of power edging toward madness—to sing a message of hope, alternative possibilities, and new futures. Such singing is not a substitute for faithful action in the arenas of power and influence, but perhaps faithful singing must precede such action as acknowledgment that the Spirit that drives out envy, anger, and fear comes from the God who is with us, and not from our power alone.

In the painting Saul holds the spear. He has not used it yet, but he will later use it in an attempt to kill David even as he plays for Saul's benefit. But, the spear or sword (used as symbols in these stories of military power) will be used in David's hand to kill Goliath and eventually drive oppressors from the land. We may wish that God's purposes worked only through the harp, or that the providence of God included only benevolent spirits and not evil spirits. But God has become active in human history with all of its complexities and ambiguities. In order to move toward David God must move away from Saul and the self-serving choices he makes. The hope of the harp and the song simply reminds us that God does not leave us defenseless against troubled power. The spear will not always be held in Saul's hand.

Love and Envy

Leadership is given reality and substance in the context of circumstances and relationships. First Samuel 18 presents David and Saul as leaders who share circumstances and relationships but make different choices about them. These elements become linked into the positive portrait of David's rise to leadership.

1. David is surrounded and gifted with *love*. Six times in this chapter we are told that David is loved. Two of Saul's children love David, and that love is mentioned twice for each: Jonathan in verses 1 and 3, and Michal in verses 22 and 28. All of Israel and Judah love David (v. 16). Even Saul's servants love David, a fact Saul cynically uses to set up what he hopes will be David's death (v. 22; see also v. 5). In this chapter David does little to promote or reciprocate this love, but elsewhere we see David as compassionate, loving, and capable of deep relationships (see 1 Sam. 16:14-23; 20:1-42; 2 Sam. 1:17-27). Only distant glimpses of his public leadership in military campaigns offer any explanation of what inspires such love. Ironically Saul first loved David (16:21), but as his family, household, and all Israel come to love him, Saul no longer can. This may be an important clue to the character of Saul.

2. The love David receives is coupled with the *success* he achieves. This chapter is preceded by David's victory over Goliath (17:1-58). Four times in the chapter we are told that David was successful: as a warrior (v. 5), in all his undertakings (v. 14), in the eyes of Saul (v. 15), and especially against the Philistines, which led to his fame (v. 30). David's success comes primarily in accomplishing what Saul had been anointed and commissioned to do—bring deliverance from the Philistines. To observe that Saul saw this success (v. 15) is to note his bitter recognition of David's effectiveness and, by implication, his own failure. At least this seems to be Saul's reaction; he seems unable to enjoy David's successes as an expression of the leadership he has raised up and encouraged. For Saul, David's success is not reason for celebration but a motive for a plan to cause his removal. David, however, views his success as service to Saul's leadership and part of a common mission they share. The drama of the chapter builds as the obstacles Saul sets before David's success become the foundations for David's greater successes, for example, his dispatch to the battlefront (v. 13) and his offer of Michal in exchange for Philistine foreskins as the bridal price (vv. 24-27).

3. The picture of the love and success that come to David is built up through the events and personalities reported in narratives of public and court life. However, this narrative detail leads to a theological conclusion. David is not only loved and successful, but *the Lord is with him*. Twice this theological comment provides an explanation for the unfolding events (1 Sam. 18:12, 14). It repeats a key theme introduced in 16:18 and continued throughout the narratives of the rise of David (see the concluding affirmation in 2 Samuel 5:10). The theme appears a third time in this chapter, to record Saul's own realization that "the LORD was with David" (v. 28). Saul, along with the reader, is forced to recognize that within the human events narrated here there is a divine intention at work. God's future for Israel includes David, and that future will not be denied.

Saul loves David (16:21), draws him into his household, and could have chosen to rejoice in his military success. He could have viewed David's growing success as a partnership of leadership joined together for the sake of the kingdom. But this is not the choice Saul makes.

1. Over against the celebration of David in 1 Samuel 18 a dark counterdrama unfolds for Saul. When the women sing praises to

David more extravagantly than to Saul (v. 7), Saul's response is *anger* (v. 8) and an "eyeing" of David (v. 9) that must be interpreted as "envy" or "jealousy." Most of Saul's actions throughout the chapter express this anger and jealousy. Saul once loved David (16:21), but at the end of this chapter the final verdict is that "Saul was David's enemy from that day forward" (v. 29). The progression of Saul's actions against David throughout the chapter is a testimony to the corrosive power of envy and the anger out of which envy grows.

2. Coupled with the acting out of Saul's anger is Saul's growing *fear.* Anger and fear, as modern psychology knows, often go hand in hand. Samuel has rejected Saul as king (1 Sam. 15); now Saul's actual grip on the kingdom is slipping. Saul becomes the first to voice that the future of the kingdom is David (v. 8), although the reader has known this since Samuel's anointing of David (16:1-13). Beneath Saul's angry and hostile response to David is an escalation of fear and anxiety. "Saul was afraid of David" (v. 12). Then Saul "stood in awe of him" (a term that indicates anxiety or apprehension, v. 15). Finally, after David turns every obstacle from Saul into success, and after Saul acknowledges that "the LORD was with David," we read "Saul was still more afraid of David" (v. 29).

3. In the midst of this human drama, the narrator discerns a divine intention. For Saul this finds expression in "an evil spirit from God" that seizes him and sends him into a rage against David (v. 10). Saul's own anger and fear exemplify a deeper alienation from God and God's purposes for Israel. Saul cannot be Israel's future. His own actions demonstrate why this must be so, but the giving and withholding of God's Spirit for good or evil will make certain that it is so.

Is Saul fated to fail and David destined to succeed? Some recent treatments of this narrative have seen Saul as only, or primarily, a victim and have understood his story as one of tragic fate. David, in such a view, is destined to greatness. Both men are therefore little more than pawns in the plot of a story predetermined by the storyteller's conception of divine intention. Such a view does not do justice to the complexity of these stories. Chapter 18 offers a good example of this complexity. Before the "evil spirit from God" comes upon Saul (v. 10), he responds to the success of his own commander with anger and jealousy, seeing only danger to his throne and not benefits to his kingdom (vv. 8-9). The evil spirit that intermittently comes upon Saul does not appear responsible for Saul's actions, fating him to failure, but in this instance its presence almost seems brought on by Saul's turn to self-serving and eventually evil responses to David's success. The "evil spirit from God" does not compel Saul to evil action. Indeed, chapter 18 goes to unusual lengths to expose the inner thoughts and motives of a Saul bent on sinful protection of his own interests (see especially vv. 17, 21, 25). Anger, envy, and fear are linked in a downward spiral of spiteful and evil actions against David, who has brought nothing but benefit to the kingdom and the household of Saul. The narrator of these stories tells us both of the actions or motives of the human characters and of the divine purposes that can be discerned acting through and in spite of these human agents. God's purpose in these events is fated to have its way, but Saul and David may, nevertheless, choose their courses within that divine purpose. It is part of the artistic complexity and brilliance of these stories that both human action and divine intent are credible. Such excellence helps account for the appeal of these stories to those confessing communities who affirm both human freedom and divine providence. Leadership of God's people must be lived in relation to both of these realities.

By the end of chapter 18 Saul is engaged in a devious plot to end David's life, and his own life is gripped by fear and enmity. The spear is thrown at David (18:10-11), and "Saul was David's enemy from that time forward" (18:29). But the chapter did not begin that way. The escalation from the seed of anger, envy, and jealousy to Saul's eventual tragic collapse was not necessary. All of us experience occasions of unwarranted and self-serving anger—jealousy that the successes of another were not our own. What these episodes make clear is that evil and tragedy grow first from the small seeds of ordinary acts born of our own worst impulses. We cannot blame God for these acts; nor could Saul. However, God's judgment will not be absent when we act to injure others out of our own anger and envy. We may not plot murder, but there are many ways to do hostile injury—from malicious gossip to political campaigns of character assassination, from undermining another's leadership to opposition born of self-interest. Saul is a sad reminder that jealous anger is a common human experience, but whether we resolve it in repentance and reconciliation or take the escalating road to evil and madness makes all the difference.

By the same token love and success are not guaranteed by God's grace apart from acts of responsibility and commitment taken in the dailiness of our lives. Jonathan and Michal heard the same praise of David that Saul heard. Jonathan in particular could have protected his own interests jealously. What leads to "love" and "success" here, in contrast to the "fear" and "evil" that overshadow Saul's story, are simple acts: David's attention to his tasks, Jonathan and Michal's courage to love without regard to self-interest, and the women's willingness to sing in honest celebration of that which deserves celebrating. This narrative insists that God is at work in our lives, but not in a way that is separate from ordinary acts of human courage and faithfulness, or human sin and madness. Whether God is with us or we are alienated from God is not preordained. The conduct of our daily lives will signal to others what they need to know to judge us and our leadership.

The Eyes of Envy

First Samuel 18 is a story of envy that takes root and becomes an insidious obsession that leads to self-destructive behavior. But it begins so innocently! David and his troops return to Jerusalem after another dramatic victory. Women from "all the towns of Israel" come out to join the returning troops in a victory parade. They dance and sing choruses. "Saul has killed his thousands, and David his ten thousands" (18:7). King Saul watches the parade with pleasure until the words of the women's chorus rise above the din and become clear. The moment Saul realizes there are unfavorable distinctions being drawn (Saul's thousands versus David's ten thousands) the pleasure of the moment is lost. The joy of victory turns to anger; the celebration of solidarity is tainted with suspicion. "So Saul eyed David from that day on" (18:9).

Saul's envious glance is one of those details from the narrative of envy in 1 Samuel 18 that connects this story of a leader derailed with the church's traditions of moral theology. Envy gains notoriety through its appearance on the list of the seven deadly sins, a popular expression of the church's moral theology since at least the twelfth century. The restless sideward glance of envy's eyes is a perennial image in sermons and devotional writings, and in poetry, painting, and literature. Across the centuries the eyes of envy describe a behavior that disrupts social enterprise. It embodies a disease of the soul that primarily hurts the individual but, depending on that person's station in life, can also threaten the peace of the community.

From early times theologians of the practice of ministry have named the unique temptations to envy that come with church leadership. There are "wild beasts of temptation" assailing the priesthood, warns St. John Chrysostom in the fourth century, and one of them is the "greed for preferment (which more than anything else hurls the human soul to destruction)."[5] From the seventeenth century, with searing words, Richard Baxter counsels pastors against bitterness toward those colleagues who "eclipse their glory, or hinder the progress of their idolized reputation."[6] Contemporary observers caution against the "ardent desires and deadly appetites" that can misdirect legitimate ambition in ministry.[7] Contemporary codes of ethics for ministers routinely warn against the disparagement of colleagues.[8]

Whether leading Israel in 1000 BCE or the church on East Main Street today, the church leader's soul seized by envy combines an active imagination with a distorted view of reality. It is perfectly capable of inventing its own invisible and intricate system of score keeping: "Saul his thousands, but David his ten thousands." It can suffer wounds at the overheard report of an alleged competitor's victory and find solace in the rumors of a colleague's downfall.

To Resent Another's Victory

Michael sits looking through his old seminary picture directory wistfully. All those bright and promising young men, most not yet thirty, all but one white, were considered the hope of the future church. Maybe one or two were trying to escape the draft for the Vietnam War, but the rest were headed for decades of service as pastoral leaders in the local church. They would be, in seminary vogue of those years, "pastoral directors" who would help the "mainline church" build on its post–World War II boom.

Of course they would have to pay their dues and start at the bottom rung of the system in small churches with dwindling congregations where the budget is sustained through a steady stream of oyster dinners and candy Easter egg sales. They would attach themselves to mentors, successful pastors with wide reputations who had been proved over the long run. They would offer their services to the denomination's boards and causes. It would require endless mind-numbing meetings and compete with responsibilities back in the local church, but also provide important connections and occasions for face recognition.

So, slowly, steadily, cream rises. Like most pastors Michael could not admit to ambition, but he quietly carried some version of a life dream just the same. He expected to be serving a midsized church by his midthirties and a large church or judicatory position by fifty.

But it didn't happen that way. The landscape of the church was changing around him and the composition of clergy leadership began to register that change. The seminaries were equipping and the church was ordaining women and persons of other races and ethnic groups, not to mention second career persons. Denomination officials were singling out promising young persons, many who were neither white nor male, as well as skilled second career persons, and placing them on fast tracks. Somewhere in his midfifties Michael realized that those tracks went past his front door but did not stop there. Again and again he watched persons barely half his age, with lesser gifts and none of his proven experience, promoted before him. Michael's life dream began to dissipate. When the twice-divorced woman he had nursed to ordination only five years ago was named to a judicatory post, that life dream all but died.

Michael does not remember the particular moment when he contrived the plan to persuade some of the church's homebound members to assign their financial affairs to him. But he does remember answering some of those early pangs of guilt with an inner voice of angry alienation that surprised him. Like a daydream that grows with each iteration, the bilking scheme became ever more clever and expansive. It was only a matter of time before the juggling of accounts surpassed Michael's ability. He was almost relieved when the whole thing became public, and he was removed from his pastoral office in disgrace. Now Michael sits looking through his old seminary picture directory and sighs heavily. He wonders what became of all those bright and promising young, white men.

To Revel in Another's Defeat

Alice heard about Michael's fall from grace at a gathering of the denomination's clergy. The news both startled and fascinated her, though she was careful to wear a "what a shame" countenance and join the chorus of regret appropriate to the occasion. Alice didn't know Michael personally, only as a successful pastor and as a member of "the good ol' boy network."

Alice blamed that good ol' boy network in one guise or another for several of the more unpleasant experiences of her career. Its members were the gatekeepers who questioned her call to pastoral leadership—not to service in the church, just leadership. They were the local church interview committee that told her that of course it was fine with them if she came to be their pastor but they knew others in the congregation who would have trouble with a "woman preacher." Did she really want to have to work under those conditions? They were the colleagues who were annoyed at her requests for childcare at clergy meetings. They were the trustees who advised her to tend to the visits and leave the business of the church to the businessmen, who, by the way, were adamantly opposed to having the parsonage anywhere else but attached to the church. They were the judicatory supervisors who said they appreciated her gifts but the congregation she aspired to would demand someone with more political savvy and leadership experience.

So Alice watched her male colleagues go where she could not go, or go with an ease she could only imagine. It was the "goes without saying" decisions that bothered her most. The battles over the ordination of women may have been won, but the battles for equal recognition were far from over.[9] Anyone who knew Alice's story would not be surprised at her lack of sympathy for the career tragedies of her male counterparts. One man's loss could be another woman's opportunity. Alice tried to imagine how she might look in the massive, elevated pulpit of Michael's church, and she liked what she saw.

"An Evil Spirit from God"

One of the most troubling details from the narrative of envy in 1 Samuel 18 is the account of "an evil spirit from God" rushing upon and seizing Saul (18:9-10). Saul becomes a raving madman. He picks up a spear and goes after the unsuspecting David, who is occupied playing the lyre. Saul intends to pin him to the wall. An "evil spirit from God"? Was Saul fated to the envy that became a murderous obsession? Was he a pawn in the hands of this evil spirit sent from the very same God who once called him to leadership?

The consensus of biblical scholarship, past and present, is that Saul must bear responsibility for both the final misery of his vocation and a string of poor decisions along the way.[10] The story could have and should have turned out differently. But that consensus also recognizes the complexity of the stories of Saul, a complexity signaled in the envy narrative by the report of the descent of the evil spirit. The evil spirit may express a divine resignation to the direction Saul is taking. It may express a divine complicity that brings closure to Saul's reign and clears the way for David's leadership. It certainly points to moments in Saul's life when the power for conscious decisions was diminished and he was subject to emotional hijacking.

First Samuel 18 is more than a morality tale or a warning to not repeat Saul's mistake. There is a recognition that envy is not only about what the loser does in losing or the winner does in winning, but about the larger mystery that encompasses them both. The story is laced from beginning to end with uncontrollable elements, surprising turns, and interwoven destinies. Why does God seem to smile on the work of one leader and not, or not as much, on the work of another? What is this force that comes between leaders, unraveling their solidarity and handicapping their common cause? Why is it so hard for leaders to bless the lives they have been given rather than curse the ones they haven't? What invisible barrier prevents them from taking pleasure in the good that comes to another?

The text pushes us to a less moralistic, less voluntaristic reading of envy. That means the text may force us beyond the present main-stays of the church's moral theology and its theology for the practice of ministry in search of broader perspectives on envy. Three illustrations from the available repertoire might help.

Donald Capps casts the church's tradition of the seven deadly sins as developmental issues by relating them to Erik Erikson's eight stages of the life cycle. He associates envy with the developmental struggle of elementary school age (five to twelve): industry versus inferiority. At this stage children have a heightened sense of inferiority, some of it related to inadequate resolution of earlier conflicts, some to lack of preparation for school life, and some to the novel reality of classmates with superior academic, athletic, or social skills. The critical need for a child at this stage is to find self-expression that builds self-confidence. The danger is that the envious person then (or later in life) will become immobilized for healthy ambition by an overriding sense of inferiority.[11]

Henry Fairlie draws attention to the role of capitalism in creating and sustaining a culture of envy. First comes the pervasive advertising that attempts to generate needs and the expectation of fulfilling those needs. Then comes the subversive reduction of individual worth to ownership, the child of God reconstituted as "the con-sumer." And finally add the agitating awareness that other con-sumers have what we do not. The stage is set for the sideward glance of envy that is both self-demeaning, in that it allows itself to be measured from such a limited perspective, and destructive of the social order because it sacrifices civic pride to competition.[12]

John Rawls views envy as an important barometer of the level of justice that prevails in a given society. How a society permits or compensates for differences in opportunity will determine the amount of envy it unleashes. Envy is a collective issue. "We envy persons whose situation is superior to ours . . . and we are willing to deprive them of their greater benefits even if it is necessary to give up something ourselves. When others are aware of our envy, they may become jealous of their better circumstances and anxious to take precautions against the hostile acts to which our envy makes us prone." Social institutions can choose whether they make social discrepancy more pronounced or not. Social institutions can address the original favored circumstances of some over others or not. A *well-ordered society will mitigate envy.*[13]

Could the church be such a well-ordered society, a place where leaders like Michael and Alice discover a connection that overpowers their temptations to resent another's victory or revel in another's defeat? Could Michael come to acknowledge the lift of white male privilege in his career to date? Could Alice look for the human face behind the "good ol' boy" label? Could they find common cause against evil spirits of envy that overrun the individual's power to resist? Is there a higher ground where the colors of Michael's and Alice's respective life dreams bleed into one?

The final solution to envy is not an asylum where each of the inmates is lost in private fantasy. The final solution is a thriving community where those who live out their inner narratives "before God" ultimately experience community because God is one and God is able to orchestrate the unique energy of each individual's experience of providence. The reign of God is a party where the elder brother of the prodigal son does in fact go inside and join the revelry (Luke 15:11-32). In Jeremy Taylor's vision of the soul purged of its sin and ready to meet its maker, the envious man "gives God hearty thanks for the advancement of his brother."[14] But on the way to that community, hard questions of social recognition, equal opportunity, and structures of competition must be asked continually.[15] They must be addressed by all church leaders, but especially by those called to judicatory positions with more power to intervene in the corporate culture. The contribution of secular leadership studies to this intervention should not be overlooked. Sometimes the biggest obstacle to just community in the church is its own rhetorical mystification of the issues.[16]

Concentration

Is there any point where Saul's downward spiral of envy could have been checked? Granted that the sideward glances, the tendency to slant the truth of events, the bouts of cancerous paranoia all have a way of adding up to a point of no return, were there opportunities for Saul to choose an alternate destiny before that point was reached? First Samuel offers glimpses of three such opportunities. First, there is Saul's response to the healing power of music (16:14-23). At least for the time that Saul surrenders to the melody of the lyre he is lifted above his brooding obsessions. The identity of the lyre player, David, will soon close that door. Second, there is the witness of Saul's adult children. Michal actively intervenes to save David from her father's murderous envy (19:11-17), and Jonathan becomes an active advocate for David in his father's presence (19:1-7). Yet Saul seems incapable of receiving these words and deeds as coming from grown-ups worthy of respect. And third, after Saul's envy has forced David to become a fugitive on the run, there are episodes where David overtakes Saul unaware, has the opportunity to kill him, but spares his life (24:1-22). After one occasion Saul even seems to have a conversion: "Now I know that you shall surely be king, and that the kingdom of Israel shall be established in your hand" (24:20). But the change of heart is short-lived.

Nothing seems to break the spell. Saul becomes so mesmerized by David's good fortunes that he suffers a fundamental loss of concentration. He forgets the unmerited favor of God that smiled on him as a youth. He develops a convenient blindness toward the everyday faithfulness of God and others, the background grace that provides lift to his life. He misses cues and loses his place in the unfolding script of what God intends to do in forming a people to be a blessing to the nations. He forfeits playful trust and surrenders step by step to a brooding obsession until the obsession proves his undoing. By the end of the story Saul has become an evil man and the exercise of responsible leadership has shifted to David. Bruce Birch reminds us that even then Saul had the residual freedom to allow the throne to pass to David peaceably but chose the path of bitterness and violence.[17]

So first things first: leaders must attend to the "good enough" life stories in which they find themselves and concentrate on the projects they have been given. To put it that way, the way of biblical realism, rather than the way of the self-help brand of leadership with its entrepreneurial formulas, acknowledges that there are always elements beyond personal control. Creation is good and trustworthy but seasoned liberally with contingencies, events that "may occur but [are] not likely or intended."[18] A sudden turn of health cuts short one person's career but opens a door of opportunity for someone else. The winds of political climate shift, making a certain style of leadership unseasonable and another very appealing. Sweeping currents of history overwhelm best-laid plans. A multinational corporation with headquarters in a far away place decides to close the factory that is the economic lifeline of the community, and suddenly half of the church members are unemployed. The pastoral leader steeped in church growth must begin to ponder questions of institutional survival and triage.

Some of the things that are experienced as beyond personal control can and should be addressed, such as inequities of opportunity or the pervasive impact of a culture of honor and shame. But even here the benefit is often oblique to the effort. The pastor who devotes her energies to helping women break through the glass ceiling of leadership may only get to watch the victory at a distance. The judicatory leader who tries to change the corporate culture of a group of clergy from autonomy to collegiality may not see the harvest until an entire generation leaves the field in retirement.

Leadership is lived out in this setting. The ebb and flow of leadership credibility is experienced in this setting. The comedic rise of dark horses and tragic fall of shining stars are played out in this setting. David comes along—bright, young, politically attractive—and the fickle spotlight of public attention strays from Saul. And in this setting the leader, more often a Saul than a David, must turn to the work he or she has been given. It is a discipline of concentration.

Keeping a journal of some sort helps, even if only a calendar with brief annotations. It is a way of separating the moments of time and allowing some to stand above others. A record of the past helps connect the dots, helps uncover an overarching meaning among discrete actions and experiences. Against the seasons of the year and the seasons of the liturgical calendar the leader discerns a direction or at least a next step. It is Lent, a time to work in the language of self-abandonment and the cross, a time to pray, "not as I will, but as you will." The leader gradually concludes it is time to leave behind a congregation that seems resistant to his every initiative.

It is Advent and the pastor, who is herself "great with child," finds new dimensions of hope in the scripture she opens for her lethargic congregation as together they slouch toward Bethlehem. Pastoral leaders reach conviction over a "month of Sundays," internalize the highs and lows of seasonal church attendance, and seek Easter in their marriages and careers.[19] And when they slow down long enough to look back, they sense direction. *Something's* happening; there is movement!

But the kind of concentration that overcomes the temptation to envy must have a forward dimension, too. *A church leader must have the confidence to dramatize his or her present life.* The confidence issue is that a particular life does matter even in the grand scheme of things. The pastor who routinely reminds parishioners that the hairs of their head are numbered and no prayer is too small must take the healing medicine he prescribes for others. There is a point where a leader must insist that the story he is living, however embryonic, amateur, or common by others' standards, is "good enough." It deserves attention.

In that story the leader is the main character sharing the stage with a cast of interesting characters, some of them saints or villains, most in between. Plots and subplots with interesting twists arise. Who knows from where, they just do.[20] In these plots there are painful setbacks and, every once in awhile, clear victories inducing joy. This daily inner narration takes place in front of an imagined audience: God, spouse, closest colleagues, or revered mentor. Sometimes it spills out in the open as when the leader lost in the reverie of that narration emits a loud "yes!" out of the blue. Most of the time it is kept in check, a quiet source of energy to be shared with a select few. In the same way that church leaders must protect the "soul of the congregation" against unfair comparisons to some Real Church as described by theologians, consultants, or bureaucrats,[21] church leaders must protect their souls, this daily inner narrative, from flippant devaluation.

The playful borrowing of management language along the way fuels this exercise of imagination. A church leader happens upon a secular study that gives a heroic vision of the manager as one who "works at an unrelenting pace," engages in activities "characterized by brevity, variety, and discontinuity," and is oriented more toward action than toward reflection. The account lifts up the pragmatism of good managers, their sensitivity to context, their adaptability, their focus on outcomes, and their openness to uncertainty. The church leader gathers such words to justify a frantic pace and validate an attention to naming issues, articulating goals, and celebrating incremental successes however small.[22] Of course church leaders live and die by attendance and giving figures! Of course they borrow freely and loosely from the metaphors of the market economy to describe their work. Those who criticize them for this practice often underestimate a healthy church leader's capacity for play in analogies.

Even upon church leaders what 1 Samuel identifies as "an evil spirit from the Lord" (envy) sometimes descends. But the case study of Saul's descent contains glimmers of alternative endings, and Dante's envious soul is in Purgatory not Inferno. There is hope. On the way to God's preferred future church leaders can choose to invest in the stories where they find themselves. They can live out the dramas they have been given. Occasional use of blinders to the fortunes of others cannot be ruled out. Concentration is everything. To paraphrase Rebbe Zusia in the Hasidic tale, on the Day of Judgment Saul will not be asked why he was not David. He will be asked only why he was not Saul.[23]

CHAPTER FIVE

SET APART

1 Samuel 20:1-42
*But if my father intends to do you harm, the LORD do so to
Jonathan, and more also, if I do not disclose it to you, and
send you away, so that you may go in safety. May the
LORD be with you as he has been with my father. (20:13)*

G od calls persons to church leadership and, ready or not, they
are lifted to a conspicuous place where even the most tena-
cious of loyalties must relinquish their grip. Mature church
leaders willingly serve as "first among equals" for a season—and in
the end, it's always only for a season. With the occasional exception—for example, Orthodoxy—church polities do not require a
second and distinct call to supervisory leadership beyond the general
call to church leader-ship. Any person called to church leadership
may be asked or appointed to assume larger responsibilities of over-
sight in the church for a season.[1]

Persons who have submitted to the call to be set apart for leadership are a pleasure to watch in action. They deftly balance partisan
pressures and a vision for the common good. They surround themselves with strong and trustworthy advisors but do not hide behind
those advisors when a decision has to be made. They listen for the
voices on the margin. They love the people warmly but endure
whatever tension may be required to keep the people focused on
their adaptive issues. They have accepted those moments of arid isolation that accompany all church leadership at one time or another.
They do not stand apart as those who overestimate their leadership

role and hold their constituents in contempt. They do not stand apart as those who have been bruised by political battles to the point of withdrawal. They stand apart as persons following a clearly understood discipline that flows from the call to church leadership.

In a certain congregation a clash of cultures has erupted and the pastor finds herself right in the middle of the tension. A young church member who lives in the local housing project behind the church parking lot claims he has heard God's call to ministry and asks for the congregation's endorsement. He has spent the last few months of his unemployment completing a junior college certificate. His "country boy" grammar and pronunciation grate on the well-educated ears of the congregation. His wife is given to uncouth language. His children are unruly by middle-class standards. He recounts his call to ministry in emotionally charged, simplistic language. As far as the congregation is concerned, he does not walk, talk, act, or feel like one of them. They are not inclined to give to him the endorsement he seeks. Why would God call somebody like *that* into ministry?

It would be so easy for the pastor to participate in the congregation's collective dismissal of the young man. After all she is more like the members of the congregation than like him. But she summons her strength and resists their collective prejudice. When the time is right she begins to counter it in casual conversations and public meetings. The pastor knows that this congregation and the denomination of which it is a part (United Methodist) have lost their connection with persons on the lower rungs of the economic ladder. This young man irritates as only a repressed memory trying to surface can. Against the tide the pastor argues for the legitimacy of the young man's call and gently coaxes the congregation to question the constrictions of its class-consciousness. She prevails. The young man is endorsed by the congregation and launched on a successful career of pastoral ministry marked by a special capacity to work across class divisions.

An African American bishop serves in a rural area that is 98 percent Caucasian. He experiences incidents of prolonged and inexplicable neglect at restaurants. He has close encounters with aggressive drivers in pickup trucks along desolate mountain roads as he visits from church to church. Sometimes in meetings there are outbursts of anger over one of his decisions that end a hair's breath away from a racial slur. When he walks down the streets of small towns he often feels those Neighborhood Watch stares. And there are all those episodes of exaggerated deference at public gatherings where whites, hoping to show peers how progressive they are, engage him in artificial conversation.

The bishop shares his worst moments with a small group of colleagues and intimates. He ponders those experiences and reworks them until they come out in his preaching as poignant illustrations of human need and God's grace, until they come out cleansed of personal rancor and mercifully obtuse in the details. He turns personal injury to gospel; he models a love that is not easily offended. He holds the people of God in his heart even while the people of God keep provoking ancient fears and hatreds in his mind. He leads.

A pastor is sent to a three-point charge knowing that one of the congregations has passed the point of viability. The judicatory official says to the pastor, "We don't force anybody to do anything; they'll have to decide for themselves." There are only a handful of struggling elderly members in that church. When they are not dreaming of yesterday's glory, they are consumed in relentless fund-raising activities to keep the doors open.

As a group the church members plow forward with grim determination, but individually they share their fatigue with their pastor. It is up to the pastor to break the spell of the official optimism and the code of silence around the hard questions of mission. The pastor does this with quiet persistence. He arranges visits to the vital worship of the other two churches on the charge. He paints a vision of an abandoned church building used as a community center. He works through the polity and legal arcana that envelop the process of selling a church and transferring title. Only a couple of curmudgeons grumble behind his back. The judicatory official observes, "We should have done this a long time ago." And the congregation surrenders the desperate remains of its corporate soul to the greater mission of Jesus Christ.

There may be church leaders born to such self-differentiated identity and independent action, but for most persons the set-apart character of leadership is and will remain one of the foremost challenges. Contemporary manuals of leadership with their bravado quips from titans of sports, industry, or military do not capture the human struggles all leaders face, especially at the beginning of their vocations. Those who have been schooled in the realism of the Bible, who have been shaped by stories like David and Jonathan, know that the tug of the call and the tug of the heart may contradict, sometimes to the point of tragedy. They know that the call from God to lead the people of God, whatever its blessings, can be an early and constant source of relational stress and grief. Behind the confident presence that eventually emerges lie poignant stories like the one in 1 Samuel 20.

Listening to the Books of Samuel

The story of David and Jonathan is considered one of the great stories of friendship, both in the Bible and in all of literature. Jonathan loved David "as his own soul" (18:1, 3), and David loved Jonathan "as his own life" (20:17). Modeled here is a friendship that chooses depth of intimacy and commitment that was not a given responsibility of family or social position. It was grounded in covenant between the two and was practiced through the loyalty each gave to and claimed from the other.

Yet, the story of David and Jonathan is also a story of leadership and the ambiguity and strains put on relationships by the demands of that leadership. David's emergence as leader was a constant source of relational stress and grief. There were episodes of growing apart, of rivalries, of partisan conflicts, of old loyalties challenged by new and broader loyalties, and finally of painful conflicts between personal ties and the realities of God's call to leadership.

The danger here, of course, is that we may give in to a romantic sentimentality about friendship or other relationships and wax eloquent about all of the positive virtues of love, commitment, and loyalty as if they operated in isolation from the historical, social, and even theological contexts where leadership is exercised and makes its demands. In our haste to affirm the importance of human connectedness we overlook the ways in which leadership necessarily sets us apart. It is perhaps significant and thought-provoking that our most poignant story of friendship in the Bible does not end happily ever after. Perhaps this helps us guard against rendering the important truths of this story in the pastels of a Madison Avenue commercial.

At this point in David's story his time in the court of Saul is over. Saul's jealousy has now led to attempts on David's life, and Saul's own children, Michal and Jonathan, have helped David escape (1 Sam. 19). David does not dare return, because Saul will kill him. David is a fugitive, and yet the story knows and anticipates that he will be the one to lead Israel into the future rather than Jonathan, the crown prince. Jonathan not only helps David escape but pledges loyalty to David, a loyalty that transcends the circumstances that divide them and recognizes that David is set apart by God for a purpose that goes beyond Jonathan's own personal self-interest. David and Jonathan enter separate paths of service in leadership but do not let the divergence destroy the integrity of their commitment to one another.

A key theological term in this episode is the Hebrew word *hesed,* which is difficult to translate adequately. It appears often in connection with Israel's covenant with God, where it is used frequently to describe God's covenant love and loyalty. It has often been translated as "steadfast love," "loving-kindness," or "mercy." In this passage, both David and Jonathan appeal to this concept, translated in the NRSV as "deal kindly" (v. 8), and "faithful love" (vv. 14, 15). The NIV uses "kindness" for all three occurrences. Much of the research on this key word suggests that the term really indicates both the attitude and action of "loyalty" in relationships.

This is a story of conflicting claims of loyalty. The conflict is between the familial and the covenantal, between relationship and the call to leadership. Jonathan has responsibility as a son to his father, and, for that matter, David, too, has obligations as a son-in-law to Saul. But Saul's intent to kill David places family loyalty in conflict with a covenant made between Jonathan and David (18:3; 20:8, 16) and with David's call to replace Saul in leadership. The conflict of loyalties also occurs between the personal and the political. The "love" (18:1, 3; 20:17) and "loyalty" (20:8, 14, 15) between David and Jonathan are not limited to their personal and intimate relationship. Both terms also reflect sociopolitical loyalties and commitments related to leadership in Israel. Jonathan and David both understand that beyond their personal future the political future of Israel is at stake. Saul angrily insists that Jonathan's political interests as heir to the throne require that he set aside the shameful choice of personal commitment to David (vv. 30-31). Jonathan knows that his loyalty to David is not simply to a friend but to one who will be king instead of him, and he asks of David loyalty as king and not just as friend (vv. 13-16). From the beginning of their relationship, when we read of Jonathan's love for David (1 Sam. 18:1, 3), Jonathan gives David his own robe, tunic, sword, and belt (v. 3). These possessions are not merely personal gifts but are the tokens of rule that identify Jonathan as the heir to the throne. By this act Jonathan acknowledges David as Israel's future leader, and in so doing he himself sows the seeds of tension between their personal relationship and the commitments of leadership of God's people. David, even as Jonathan loves him, is set apart.

Some have seen Jonathan in chapter 20 choosing exclusively for David and against Saul. This is true, in a sense. Jonathan not only supports and protects David against the wrath of his father, but he seems to see the most clearly of anyone in the story that David represents God's future for Israel. He alone gives voice to the recognition that God is working through David in these events (vv. 12, 14, 16, 22, 23, 42). In a sense Jonathan chooses for the Lord, not just for David. But this choice is not allowed to be absolute and unambiguous. Jonathan must, for the sake of loyalty to David, oppose his father and risk his father's violence (v. 33), but he refuses to abandon his father or the demands of familial loyalty. He knows his father, Saul, is doomed; he knows David is Israel's future. He can protect that future, but he cannot participate in it. In this chapter the word "father" is used fourteen times, emphasizing the painful relationship that Jonathan cannot escape. Saul is his father. He loves David, but he does not go with him. He stays with Saul at some personal risk and with the knowledge that he is doomed with him. In the end he dies fighting with his father in a battle that could not be won (31:2). It is little wonder that David, who better than anyone knows of Jonathan's loyalty, can sing on hearing of the death of father and son, "Saul and Jonathan, beloved and lovely! In life and in death they were not divided" (2 Sam. 1:23*a*).

The bittersweet story of David's friendship with Jonathan, the son of the man he will replace in leadership, richly captures the *potential cost to relationships* of answering the call to leadership. David can no longer choose his actions as a purely personal matter once he has been anointed to lead God's people. The path to leadership can be costly and will force choices that would not be our preference on a purely personal basis. There is a personal cost to the decision to accept God's call to serve others in leadership. David cannot escape the path that sets him apart from Jonathan unless he chooses to refuse the call to become Israel's king.

But this story teaches not only of cost to those set apart but of the possibility of having relationships that deepen and become richer even in the face of such costs. Leadership does not demand that we isolate ourselves from relationship, only that we recognize these potential costs. The story of friendship between David and Jonathan suggests that love and loyalty always are experienced in the midst of ambiguous claims and responsibilities. The experience of friendship and relationship can lead to painful as well as fulfilling decisions. In our societal context we are prone to cheap relationships. Many live under the illusion that their own self-fulfillment and self-gratification are the primary goals of relationship. But pursuit of such shallow relationships can never result in the experience of loyal, mutual friendship and would never be worthy of those truly called to lead. Loyalty requires honoring commitments, recognizing claims beyond the self, expressing concern for the other as fully as for self, parting as well as being with, giving rather than grasping, experiencing pain along with joy.

Leadership *subjects our personal covenants to the claims of obedience to God's broader purposes for our lives.* The love and loyalty in the friendship of Jonathan and David surely had deep personal dimensions, as the moving scene of their final parting demonstrates. But at every point in the story it is clear that these two friends knew that their commitment had implications for the future of God's kingdom. God's call to serve the kingdom sets a broader horizon within which our personal relationships take on new meaning. It is a meaning that must recognize the existence of that broader horizon.

This story points to God as guarantor of all our loyalties. Over and again, largely in the voice and witness of Jonathan, we are reminded that loyalty in human relationships finds its full meaning in commitment made in the name of the Lord. It is trust that the future is

God's future that makes pain and ambiguity endurable. It is the hope that God's future will come that allows us to risk challenging the vested interests and human cowardice that, in the name of stability and convention, undermines loyalty and love. Jonathan could choose against his own self-interest and his father's restricted vision of the future because his horizon was God's future. His vision encompassed more than the present realities of a homicidal father, a fugitive friend, risky intercession, and tearful parting. Beyond these events Jonathan could see God's future for Israel, and David could respond in loyal commitment, even to Jonathan's descendants, trusting that God's future would come. In the complexities of our own relationships, our horizons are often too limited to the human possibilities that seem available in the present moment. One of the functions of this text, and of the church that reads it, is to offer the horizon of God's future as hopeful possibility to those who struggle to see past the pain and ambiguity of present circumstance—to suggest that there is a larger vision that our relationships can serve. Those who would offer loyal friendship and faithful relationship in the midst of life's struggles must relinquish self-interest and risk painful struggle not only for the sake of the other in the relationship but for the future of leadership of God's kingdom that such loyalty makes possible.

To be set apart for leadership is not a call to be isolated and lonely, but a call to recognize our connection to God as the defining element in our lives. David is so certain of his connection with God that he dares to use the holy bread for secular purposes (1 Sam. 21); he dares to live with the Philistines, Israel's enemies (1 Sam. 27). Set apart, he is able to break the taboos of the community for the sake of leading the community. He has the freedom to honor relationships while nevertheless charting the course of God's call into a new future, as when he spares the life of Saul out of honor and respect yet continues on toward the leadership that will supplant Saul (1 Sam. 24 and 26). In the end, David's freedom as "a man after God's own heart," a man set apart to lead Israel, allows him to fulfill the vow of loyalty, love, and friendship he made to Jonathan, "The LORD shall be between me and you, and between my descendants and your descendants, forever" (1 Sam. 20:42). Probably against the advice of his political counselors, David welcomes the lame son of Jonathan,

Mephibosheth, to his household and his table in fulfillment of the vow to his friend (2 Sam. 9). The grandson of his sworn enemy, the son of his sworn friend, is welcomed to the house of David, the leader set apart to bring a new future to God's people. It is as set apart leaders that we too can model a loyalty in relationships that is not based on self-interest but on the loyalties of love, justice, and mercy, a loyalty that is willing to bear the cost of leadership for the sake of God's wider purposes.

The Tug of the Heart

Before David is the confident and resolute leader of the troops he is the weeping friend in the embrace of Jonathan. The fork in the road moment is here. As much as David loves Jonathan he must abandon him for the sake of a larger public destiny. And as much as Jonathan loves David he must remain with his father and play out the dismal script of a tragic ending. As the commentary points out, 1 and 2 Samuel do not offer such moments as a case study to be garnered for instruction against making similar mistakes. The books of Samuel offer such moments to us as if to say, this is the way life really is.

This is the way it really is: leadership subjects our personal covenants to the strain of the larger human drama. Leadership exacts relational stress and grief. Along the path to leadership we are caught up in fiercely competitive contests that create winners and losers. We must break with emotionally gripping tribal loyalties for the sake of the larger common good. And as careful as we may be, we find ourselves swept along by a tide of larger forces, playing our part, even though the part we play ruptures the ties of family or friendship, sometimes beyond repair in this lifetime. There is a distinctive voice in much of the contemporary leadership literature, particularly in the secondary leadership literature that appears outside an academic setting. It borders on the voice of Batman comics with strong verbs and short sentences, with instant transitions and action without resonance. Pow! Bang! Zap! If we try hard, most of us in church leadership still can remember our first jarring encounter with that literature. We came to it as persons immersed in the theological voice of compound sentences, nuances of tense, and the use of circumlocutions for God. And we encountered these passionate books that avoided four syllable words, presented truth in aphorisms, and eschewed debate with the theological community in footnotes. The authors of these works did not pause for theological subtleties, and they made us feel effete for doing so. They took special delight in lists of bold phrases that allegedly stand above all contexts like the Ten Commandments. The more articulate writers of these books had a name for this new voice in the literature of leadership. It was the voice of a "scientific revolution," it was the economy of style released by a new "paradigm shift."[2]

At no point is the new leadership literature less reticent or more curt than in its treatment of those who would resist the leader's vision and direction. For a couple of decades church leadership literature has paraded before us a variety of stereotypical opponents, sometimes even assigning them names that resonate with their alleged roles. Martha the Mistress of Trivial Pursuit belongs to the GI generation (too often another careless label) for whom official membership in the organization counts more than participation in ministry. Richard the Reactionary has seen a lot of changes in the church in his lifetime. He has been against every one of them! These stereotypes of resistance to church growth are never described as developed characters in a rich textured story, but only as caricatures as if lifted from a medieval morality tale. This same church leadership literature has a tendency to label whole groups of persons according to their alleged function in the organization: the Old Guard, the Obstructionists, the Censors, and sometimes, when it gets nasty, the Pharisees.

The best-case scenario is that church leaders who read such literature find playful humor in such labeling and have the good sense not to apply it too closely to their congregations. The reality is that some leaders will use this literature with its distortion of truth to fuel their growing sense of alienation from the congregation. The narrative of a leader and the people must reflect the complexities and subtleties of a healthy and well cared for covenant. When the prevailing narrative becomes that of the bruised leader alone the covenant is in jeopardy. Corporate vision and forward action are even less likely. And when those who resist the leader's interpretation of reality are dismissed as caricatures of resistance, how can they be the object of the love the leader carries in his or her heart for God's people?

The leader of God's people filled with compassion but doing the hard thing anyway is the preferred image of church leadership. "David wept the more" (1 Sam. 20:41) at the clash of personal and public covenants and, so must we. Church leaders never have the luxury of stepping outside their vocation of pastoral ministry. In practice that means the man who spoke passionately against your salary increase two nights ago at the board meeting may need your visit in the hospital this afternoon after suffering a heart attack. The organist who routinely scorns your attempts to condense the worship service may come seeking your help with a failing marriage as if oblivious to the professional tiffs between you. They are souls in our keeping. Calling them fools (Matt. 5:22) is never an option, not even in the torment of leadership battles.[3]

And should the call to leadership strain our personal ties to the point of rupture (and it is the witness of 1 and 2 Samuel that this will happen), the aftermath is not the occasion for vindictive glee. The pleasure of doing the right thing is always tinged with the pain of casualties along the way. This chastened memory puts all our political games in perspective. The leader was never that pure; the enemy was not that transparent. The search for grace in the aftermath of conflict must continue. Who knows? As we see in the touching footnote on Mephibosheth (2 Sam. 19:24-30) our chastened memories may even uncover future opportunities for kindness to the family members of former enemies.[4]

Surviving on Domestic Visions

The conspicuous nature of church leadership, the exhilaration, tension, and occasional pain of being "set apart" may have seemed self-evident in most seasons of the church's life, but not in ours. The church of former times might applaud the tragic resolution in 1 Samuel 20 that sends Jonathan back home and propels David onto the public arena of leadership. That church could hear the story of David and Jonathan's separation as part of a trajectory of vocational sacrifice. The trajectory extends back to the call of Abraham and

Sarah to leave country, kindred, and household and follow the Lord "to the land I will show you" (Gen. 12:1-3). It extends forward to the New Testament where Jesus the prophet of the Last Days calls disciples to leave behind their work, loved ones, and familiar surroundings.[5] The church in most seasons could locate itself in the current of that trajectory as from age to age its leaders experienced anew the call to ministry that marks, delineates, and distinguishes.

The test of vocational separation might vary from age to age, but it is always there. In one age the call to church leadership might tear persons away from the bosom of family privilege and take them to monasteries to prepare for leading a counterculture of poverty, chastity, and humility. In another age the call might carry them to universities in far away cities like Paris and London where they would be equipped for ministry by mastering a more universal language (Latin) that would free them to minister near and far. In the Reformation the call might single them out for the study of the Word to which they and their future parishioners would be subject. Among the Puritans the call demanded the autonomy from the congregation to speak plainly and reprove the saints along their journey to Zion.

The itinerant preachers of the Great Awakening had the clothes on their backs, the horses they rode, the possessions in their saddlebags, and precious little else! At their best, the missionary sons and daughters of nineteenth and twentieth centuries forsook the comforts and advantages of industrialized societies to carry faith, education, and healing to faraway places. And "mainline" Protestant sons (and eventually daughters) of the early to mid-twentieth century left the comforts of familiar surroundings for the faraway seminaries of the denomination. There they would learn a historical critical method that would initially distance them from their Sunday school faith, but in the end would equip them to help their congregations navigate the stormy seas of secularism that arose in the second half of the twentieth century.[6]

But for some reason (theological amnesia? institutional aging? xenophobia?) the contemporary church has become uncomfortable with the call to church leadership that marks, delineates, and distinguishes. The contemporary church seems driven to question almost every facet of the call that sets apart and to critique it as a symptom rather than honor it as a tradition. In the name of recovering the ministry of all Christians, some in the church even question the need for the distinctiveness of an ordained clergy. But for these persons the ministry of all Christians is not taken as a call to infiltrate commerce, education, and social policy with the values of God's reign; it is taken only as the call to revitalize a languishing church culture. In other words, to take up the work once thought restricted to clergy.[7]

Other voices in the church cast suspicion on the cloistered preparation for ministry along with its specialized knowledge and its constant attention to formation issues in the context of a seminary community. They argue that seminaries are a thing of the past and parade the theological equivalent of home schooling as the wave of the future. But preparing for church leadership is always more than preparing for a trade even if the mentoring relationship is a crucial pedagogical component. It is a tapping into the intellectual, spiritual, and emotional depths offered in a good theological education, the texts and traditions that are the foundation for ministry. The church's involvement in the enterprise of formal education is not an accidental development. It exposes persons to the larger community's discourse and challenges persons to shed parochial loyalties for the sake of larger commitments.[8]

Still others strike a populist chord, arguing that larger covenants of connection, assembly, or synod should be ignored in the name of loyalty to locale. As one congregation said when declining an interview for a prospective pastor arranged by a judicatory, "We prefer someone who became a disciple among us and was mentored right here, someone who carries our DNA." There is a quiet assumption in many circles of the church today that episcopal and presbyterian polities with their modes of "interference" in the life of the local congregation are destined to give way to congregational polity—a confidence in evolution for which there is no historical support.[9]

Of course there are pathologies in those instances where the call to church leadership more visibly sets apart persons to lead. People do "escape" to seminaries and undergo ordination in spite of screening. People do run from the give and take of a living congregation and hide behind theological abstractions or the latest plan for restructuring from denomination headquarters. There are Lone

Rangers, and some of them exploit the relative freedom from scrutiny of their ministry. They may leave behind trails of ineffectiveness, immorality, or crime.

But it is time to start questioning this questioning of the call to set apart ministry. Are there not pathologies in this direction as well? The preferences for the imminent, the affable, and the pragmatic dimensions of the call to church leadership have to register in diminished vision and vitality. Leaders who only know their local context for ministry cut themselves off from the transcending field of force available to them and to the congregations they lead. It is the field of the Spirit's work in creation and history, the outpouring of the Spirit that transcends boundaries of time or place.[10]

The church needs leaders who know that the call from God to lead the people of God can separate them from home and dampen friendships. There will be intimate and heartbreaking scenes like the parting of David and Jonathan. To follow the call to church leadership is to anticipate "breaking hearts" somewhere along the line. There are parents who wished for their children a more prestigious career. There are best friends from the first church served who were convinced their beloved friend and pastor would never agree to another assignment. There are colleagues of mythical stature who must be confronted because of their immorality.

There will be toughening up with time and practice, but the tests continue. There is the showdown with the wealthiest member of the congregation who wants to ignore the denomination's polity and is vocal about leaving if he does not get his way. There is the clash with the subversive associate who manages to rally a solid base of support. Sometimes the church leader must go out into the wilderness beyond further human counsel, regions where only wild beasts and angels attend, to fetch the hard decision or alternative vision that will unfreeze the congregation. Veterans know that the loneliest moments of church leadership are often multilayered dramas that come in mid or late career at a time when they are more attuned to the fragility of life and least prone to burn bridges behind them.

CHAPTER SIX

DUCKING SPEARS

1 Samuel 25:2-35

David said to Abigail, "Blessed be the LORD, the God of Israel, who sent you to meet me today! Blessed be your good sense, and blessed be you, who have kept me today from bloodguilt and from avenging myself by my own hand!" (25:32-33)

The church is never a more peculiar people than when it points to the alternative of the peaceable reign of God. The surrounding culture offers violence as titillating news and entertainment; the church struggles to make sense of its "texts of terror" and talks about the things that make for peace. The surrounding culture offers mesmerizing images of power without conscience, injury without emotional resonance, and destruction without repercussions. The church answers from its ample repertoire of counterimages: crucifixion and martyrdom, swords turned into plowshares, lions and lambs grazing together while a child plays amid them. The surrounding culture rushes to meet the violence of September 11, 2001 with tears of compassion and a call for action. The church rushes to meet the violence of September 11, 2001 with tears of compassion and a call for action, but the church's call is tempered by its theological traditions of pacifism and just war.

The church leader stands before the people of God as translator of the peaceable reign of God and as defender of its counterimages and theological traditions. In some historical moments this only requires the church leader to articulate the finer and dominant impulses of the congregation. But there are moments when the church leader may be at serious odds with much of the congregation. The willingness to say an honest word about violence, especially violence officially sanctioned, is one of the church leader's hardest tests.

Before the church leader is an advocate for the peaceable reign of God, the church leader is a citizen of that reign in the ongoing life of the congregation. Before the church leader preaches or teaches the hard truths of power, injury, and proportionate response, the church leader lives them out in multiple tests of anger. What will he do with that curmudgeon who opposes every church growth strategy he suggests? How will she respond when the personnel committee refuses even to discuss her request for continuing education support? When does he quit turning the other cheek at the blatant disregard for his office by someone who keeps comparing him unfavorably to his predecessor?

Sweet Revenge

Like the young David the church leader may go along for some time ducking the spears of adversaries, cloaked in the innocence of inexperience and lacking the social capital to do battle. But like David in the story of Nabal and Abigail there will come a day when it is no longer necessary for the church leader to duck spears because the church leader is now the one holding them. The leader, spear in hand, is a harder image for church leaders to own than the image of ducking the thrown spears. We are not particularly comfortable viewing ourselves as agents with the power to do harm. Our self-image is that of a pastoral presence dwelling among the people of God, and we generally dislike confrontation.

If we did struggle at all with the subject of power in our theological training it was only power at a distance. Perhaps we studied power as a formal attribute of God or as a tool in a liberation critique. We studied God's power as one side of the theodicy triangle that needed to be balanced with knowledge and love. We raised questions about the implications of God's omnipotence. Or, in the other direction, we studied the power of oppressive social structures and arrangements that were disguised as theological truth and were being unmasked by liberation or feminist theologians such as James Cone, Elisabeth Schüssler Fiorenza, and Justo González. What we did not get around to doing in our seminary work was to study the actual power employed in the day to day work of leading the church.

We did not connect abstract theological concepts with concrete political realities in the everyday life of the congregations we would be serving.

This curious contradiction—the church leader bearing the power to do harm while simultaneously unaware of or even denying that power—is a formula for trouble. Church leaders are capable of remarkable polarities of behavior, now quiet and benign then suddenly aggressive and callous. This symptom of a passive aggressive pattern so hidden from the leader is entirely obvious to outside observers called in afterward to clean up the mess.

It looks like this. Paul did not say anything at the personnel committee meeting when, for the third year in a row, they neglected to give him a cost of living raise. Paul was stoic about broken promises concerning the overgrown azalea bushes crowding the front walk to the parsonage and the mold problem in the basement where the laundry appliances were located. Paul smiled unflinchingly when a prominent family informed him they had invited the beloved former pastor to come back and perform their daughter's wedding next July.

Years passed and things began to turn at the church, new shoots of growth sprung up, new energy for mission surfaced, and a grudging recognition for Paul's special gifts of leadership began to surface. The church was at a critical point in its life, on the verge of voting to build a huge family life and worship center, when Paul "struck back," though he would never use that term to describe it. To the shock of the congregation and the dismay of the building committee Paul announced that he had been "called" to another congregation faraway and would be leaving town in one month. Paul could barely contain the smugness in his voice each time he told others how sorry he was to be leaving.

Listening to the Books of Samuel

One of the theological themes of the books of Samuel is that leadership in answer to God's call comes as a gift, but the temptation of those in leadership is to think that authority is something to be grasped. The power that comes through grasp almost always does violence to those the leader should serve. Chapters 24–26 of 1 Samuel focus on whether or not David will use violence in order to gain or hold power. Like Saul, David receives power as a gift. Will he, like Saul, resort to the violence that this power makes so readily available?

One of the dangers of power is its seduction to violence, whether overt or, as often in the church, subtle and manipulative. The temptation is to resort to violence as a way of gaining, maintaining, or holding on to power. The temptation is to move from gift to grasp. Saul fell victim to this temptation. Although he gained his throne not by violence, but by the gift of God, he resorts to increasing levels of violence as he feels power shifting from himself to David. Initially, as king, the balance of power is on Saul's side. As David's popularity grows, Saul first becomes violent toward David. David is forced to become a fugitive from Saul's murderous intentions. But violence tends to breed violence. Saul's paranoid grasping after his own power leads next to violent turns toward those who support David, and eventually toward those he only imagines support David. His violence is inflicted on his own son Jonathan, his own servants, and in deadliest fashion on the whole community of the priests of Nob (1 Sam. 22:6-23).

As Saul's bent to violence increases, his hold on power ironically decreases. From 1 Samuel 18 to 23 there is a shifting of power away from Saul and toward David, as one after another the witnesses to David's future kingship step forward. At the beginning of these chapters Saul is powerful and David is vulnerable, but in 1 Samuel 24–26 the situation is reversed. In chapters 24 and 26 it will be Saul who is vulnerable and David who holds power over his life and acts with compassion toward his own enemy. In chapter 25 David holds the power to seize what he needs through violence and revenge against a petty fool named Nabal, but Nabal's wife Abigail intervenes to save him from the taint of coming to the throne with blood on his hands. Leadership in God's kingdom cannot be achieved by violence. In the final speech of chapter 24, Saul himself will finally confess the knowledge that David will be king (24:20). The shift of power to David is finally complete; even Saul must acknowledge it. It is a great reversal like those foreseen in Hannah's song (1 Sam. 2:1-10). The eighth son from a family of little influence or wealth, forced to live as an outlaw and fugitive, nevertheless will be Israel's future king because he is the man after God's own heart (13:14). In this great reversal of power, David now faces the temptation to violence that power brings, and his response makes the case for leadership that refuses to resort to violence.

Chapter 24 relates an incident in which Saul's life is unexpectedly placed in David's hands. Out of respect for God's anointed David refuses to kill him as his men urge him to do. Instead he stealthily cuts off a piece of Saul's robe and confronts Saul with it. David speaks of his own innocence and compassion, and presents the evidence that he has spared Saul's life. Saul, shocked out of his madness into lucidity, confesses that he has repaid David's goodness with evil. He acknowledges that the future of Israel lies with David as king.

This episode is closely paralleled by the story in 1 Samuel 26. Most scholars believe these stories are variant accounts of the same incident. There is no agreement on which account is earlier or more authentic. In the present arrangement, the two similar episodes build a sequence (with the story of David/Nabal/Abigail in 1 Samuel 25 between them) about David facing issues of power, violence, bloodguilt, and innocence. The viewpoint of the narrator and editor of these stories as they now stand is that David refused to gain or hold power by violence. David spares Saul's life (24); he is persuaded by Abigail to spare Nabal (25); he spares Saul again (26). These become stories that allow us to reflect on the temptations of leadership to grasp power for itself rather than to receive power as the gift of God for the sake of the people. The story suggests that David models an alternative to the usual power arrangements and breaks the connection of power with violence although he must live close to its temptations. Can such an alternative response to the interconnections of power and violence be maintained?

First Samuel 25, the narrative of David's encounter with Abigail and her husband Nabal, is the second story, and perhaps the centerpiece, in this sequence of three chapters dealing with the temptation to violence that comes with power. David's innocence of such violence is demonstrated, and his coming kingship is cleared from suspicion of bloodguilt. In chapter 24 and in the similar episode in chapter 26, David restrains his impulse toward violence against Saul and twice refuses to take the life of the one who threatens his own life. Between these encounters David requires Abigail's intervention to avoid incurring bloodguilt by taking revenge on Nabal.

Chapter 25 is constructed in a way such that character and plot point beyond the narrative boundaries of the chapter. We can sketch the broad outline of some of these interconnections and will discuss details in the verse by verse comment.

The character of Nabal in this story seems to represent Saul in many details. Nabal, like Saul, is spared from the vengeful hand of David, although the intervention of Abigail is required. Nabal is also one who returns evil for good, a characteristic Saul admits about himself (24:17). Nabal's name means fool, and his actions are the marks of a fool (25:25). This identification reflects the confession Saul makes in 26:21, "I have been a fool." Nabal's response to David's request for food and drink is to treat him as a servant "breaking away" from a master (25:10). This accusation reflects Saul's treatment of David since chapter 19. Most important, Nabal's death, not by the hand of David but by the hand of the Lord, prefigures Saul's death. Abigail's speeches twice look ahead to Saul's death while also speaking of her husband. In 25:26 Abigail swears by the Lord, "Let your enemies and those who seek to do evil to my lord be like Nabal." The only one "seeking" to do evil to David outside this story is Saul. When Abigail later says "If anyone should rise up to pursue you and to seek your life" (v. 29*a*), it is impossible not to think of Saul's pursuit, which has dominated the story in recent chapters. She continues, "the lives of your enemies he [God] shall sling out as from the hollow of a sling" (v. 29*b*). Immediately we think of Goliath, vanquished by a stone from David's sling. But when Nabal is later struck dead by the Lord, the act is accompanied by the notice that "he became like a stone" (v. 37). David's enemies, whether Goliath, Nabal, or Saul, are slung out like a stone to their deaths. Both Nabal and Saul die because they opposed David, and in so doing opposed God's future for Israel.

Abigail saves David from incurring bloodguilt, but in these events we are exposed to a darker side of David's character than we have seen thus far. Although he is restrained by Abigail's timely intervention, David is willing to kill, and to do so on a major scale through the act of wiping out all the males in Nabal's household (v. 22). This side of David's character foreshadows a later time when his willingness to kill is not restrained, and he sends Uriah to his death in order to take Bathsheba for himself (2 Sam. 11). The consequences of this surrender to his own violent side will be monumental for David and his family (2 Sam. 12–20). In both incidents, David seeks to kill a man and then marries that man's wife. Due to Abigail, who acts as an instrument of the Lord, David does not kill Nabal, and the marriage will remain untainted by bloodguilt. David does kill Uriah and his marriage to Bathsheba is shadowed by blood.

Abigail is the central character in this episode that occurs in the larger context of David's coming kingship. She appears as the agent through whom the gifts of the Lord are at work to restrain David from violence. In contrast to the foolishness of Nabal, the wise Abigail recognizes David as the future king of Israel, and she understands the danger that bloodguilt would constitute to that kingship. It is through her remarkable human gifts of intelligence, beauty, excellence in speech, resourcefulness, and a willingness to take action that the word and will of God are made clear to David. David is thus enabled to step back from the danger.

Through these characters and the roles they play in this story we find an opportunity to reflect on the power that leadership brings and the temptation to use that power in ways that do violence to the very people we are called to lead in the church. The story of Abigail and David illumines several issues related to leadership in the church.

1. One of those issues is the temptation to use the power of leadership for vengeance against those perceived to be opponents or impediments. Petty, vengeful acts on the part of leaders in the church are often justified with an appeal to the noble ends being served. Paul addressed this very issue in the early church. "Beloved, never avenge yourselves, but leave room for the wrath of God; for it is written, 'Vengeance is mine, I will repay, says the Lord'" (Rom. 12:20, also Heb. 10:30). The story of Abigail saving David from bloodguilt could very easily use this line from the apostle Paul as an Aesop-like moral at the end of the story. First Samuel 25 could serve as a parable on the truth and importance of this statement by Paul. Yet, Paul is actually quoting the Torah in Deuteronomy 32:35, and this principle of reserving vengeance to God (and not taking it into one's own hands) is an important Hebrew moral principle (see also Prov. 20:22; 24:29).

This notion of vengeance as belonging to God is widely misunderstood. Many modern Christians would read Paul's statement as a remnant of some harsh, judgmental Old Testament God. God's vengeance is not an arbitrary or capricious divine wrath, but an expression of divine governance related to justice and righteousness as operative and maintained by God in the world. Even more important, the reservation of vengeance to God removes any justification for human vengeance. If "vengeance is mine, says the Lord" then it cannot be yours or mine. Both Abigail and David state the most important outcome of Abigail's intervention, namely that David did not take vengeance into his own hand (vv. 26, 33).

The forestalling of vengeance by one's own hand opens the possibilities for creative moral action and discernment of God's providence. Paul's reflection on vengeance as the Lord's is followed by the statement, "No, 'if your enemies are hungry, feed them; if they are thirsty, give them something to drink'" (Rom. 12:20). Paul quotes Jesus' teachings (Matt. 5:44; 25:35; Luke 6:27), and Abigail lives out the virtue he taught. Because of her actions to forestall vengeance new possibilities are available. Lives are saved, of course, but the future kingdom intended for Israel by God is saved as well. God does act against Nabal, but David is not tainted with Nabal's blood. With their marriage both David and Abigail claim a future that could not have been possible in the aftermath of a vengeful raid. Likewise, in the events of chapters 24 and 26, David's restraint from violence leads to Saul's concession of the kingdom, a legitimization David could never have had by killing Saul.

Leadership in the church that yields to the temptations of vengeance and does violence to others in the name of God's kingdom actually forestalls the grace by which God's kingdom always arrives. Leaders who nurture grievances and use power to resolve those grievances actually become impediments to God's kingdom. It was Abigail who saw this clearly and who persuasively moved David back onto a path of more authentic leadership that trusts in God's power rather than his own.

2. "Blessed are the peacemakers, for they will be called children of God" (Matt. 5:9). Peacemaking and acting as members of God's family are allied in this saying of Jesus. To do good rather than evil is to align our actions with what God is doing. To be

peacemakers is to seek to unite human moral agency with divine agency; Abigail models this. Her husband, Nabal, models its opposite. Evil masquerades as foolishness and leads to separation from God.

Peace in the Hebrew sense of *shalom* means wholeness and well-being. David announces such a hope for peace through his emissaries to Nabal (v. 6), but Nabal's response prevents it. To act the fool is to create brokenness. Moral disregard and self-preoccupation in response to peacemaking is evil. Saul was not inherently evil and did not begin his kingship by intending the evil use of power, but he became evil in the sense of playing the fool (which he admits in 26:21). He became one who returned evil for good (24:17) through his own foolishness.

In our own time, it is often easier to confront great forces of obvious evil (the Hitlers and Stalins, KKK and Bull Connor, apartheid and ethnic cleansing) than to confront our own mean-spirited foolishness and the evil that results. It is easy to expect peacemaking and avoidance of vengeance on the part of diplomats and Nobel–prize winners. It is more difficult to rush, like Abigail, into the breaches of daily life where foolishness provokes violence and where taking up a position between the two is risky business.

The story of Abigail is a reminder for church leaders to seek grace-filled and creative resolutions to conflict in the church. But her story is also a reminder of the need for pastors and others in formal leadership roles to listen for and respond to the wise women and men that are present in the midst of every congregation. Leaders who listen only to their own voice will miss the voice of an Abigail who may save them from their own worst impulse to misuse the power of leadership. Abigail's story urges us to a new cultivation of our listening skills in which we seek to temper our own temptations with attention to the whispers of God's grace through others around us.

3. But let us not treat Abigail simply as an advisor to leaders. Abigail is an important biblical model of moral courage and peacemaking, a model as a leader in her own right. She deals with the evil of Nabal and the danger of David in a forthright and resourceful way and at considerable risk to herself. She easily could have experienced retribution from either Nabal or David. It is significant that even as a woman of wealth and privilege the servants of the house-

hold approach her in trustful confidence. She models peacemaking in her ability to see issues at stake beyond the immediate situation, and in enabling others (here most notably David) to see the long-term consequences of immediate acts of passion and self-gratification.

In her own initiatives Abigail never loses sight of the larger movement of divine initiative, but she boldly claims a part in that providential movement. She persuasively relates present moral action to the larger vision of God's future, and dares to place herself in a position to mediate the present in light of that vision (see especially her speech in 25:26-31).

We live in a world constantly needing restraint from violence and leadership empowered by grace. We could always use more Abigails. She stands as a model in her own context for actions that avoid vengeance, make for peace, and enable God's kingdom. Our context is radically different from that of Abigail, but the tasks are no less urgent. Abigail acts boldly within the framework available to her and in so doing she shapes the future of God's kingdom. Men and women may find in her example the encouragement to act for God's kingdom in opposition to the violence of our own time. In particular, Abigail may inspire us to patterns of leadership and community that are not driven by self-interest or the prerogatives of power. She suggests to us as she did to David that God's leaders must take an alternative path to the usual ways of using power in the world. That path will be marked by the humility that constantly understands the gift of leadership and refuses the grasp that would move us from service to manipulation and violence. Fools will present themselves as impediments to leadership in the church. Abigail reminds us that dealing well with such fools is a mark of effective leadership.

Owning Anger

The books of Samuel are straightforward about the power that comes with leadership and the dangers that come with that power. They record several abuses of power and occasionally record a narrow escape from such abuse. David ducking the spears of Saul and yielding to Abigail's importuning are vital and timely images of leadership. How unfortunate that many church leaders do not draw a connection between themselves and such images.

In the first place it is hard for church leaders to own the anger they may be experiencing. Some church leaders carry the anger of unresolved family issues into the practice of ministry as a camouflaged passion. They may be very open with anger, confronting perceived antagonists by "telling it like it is" from the pulpit, but this expression of anger is more a venting from private reserves than the exercise of firm leadership. It is only about *them*, not about building up the Body of Christ.

Other church leaders wear their anger as a mien of gentle depression that is the cost of responding too affably to frustration. They take, oh so professionally, so politely, so piously, what others throw at them: the unrealistic demands, the unsubstantiated accusations, the rudeness. But the dissonance between what they are feeling and their response must exact its price somewhere, somehow. So they become closet cynics while bluffing a worldview of human agency and a gospel of divine hope.

Still other church leaders avoid facing their anger by withdrawing from the group and investing themselves elsewhere. It is a strategy gleaned from the legacy of the American experience of the church as a voluntary organization. The hold of a given denomination or church community over a person is mitigated by that person's experience of democratic institutions and the plethora of religious options.[1] It is easier to drop out than to stay and vent. Clergy groups seem especially vulnerable to this strategy. At the first sign of serious disagreement over an issue the anger avoidance techniques kick in so that by the next meeting one or another member will be missing from the table.

All leaders are open to the temptations of unmanaged anger, what Daniel Goleman calls "the seductions of anger" and "the rush of rage."[2] There are similar warnings in the church's literature on the seven deadly sins.[3] But for many contemporary church leaders anger is a challenge to self-awareness before it is a challenge to self-management. The crucial first step may be an unglamorous confession that seems to erupt from a less than ideal self. "I am mad as hell, and I am not going to take it anymore."[4]

Owning Power

What makes unacknowledged anger such a serious issue for church leaders is the same thing that makes unacknowledged anger a serious issue for all leaders: the magnitude of the power involved. But owning that power is as much a challenge to contemporary church leaders as owning their anger.

Church leaders have considerable power, and that power has remarkable resilience. No turn of events over the last fifty years has seriously diminished that power. The recovery of the church's teaching on the ministry of all Christians may blur the line between those set apart for church leadership and those who are not, but differences persist and distinctions in power are some of the clearest indicators that the line is not a mirage. The church's loss of moral voice and cultural influence, the condition named in theological discussion as "post-Christendom," may carry the assumption that the social status of clergy has eroded, but this assumption is seriously overstated. Whether church leaders become more assertive and entrepreneurial (the church growth solution) or more prophetically peculiar (the saving remnant solution), they continue to wield a power solidly supported by personal attributes and community recognition.[5]

First and foremost church leaders have *the power of their call to ministry*. There are people in the crowd who move with more resolution and act from a deeper assurance, and these people are called clergy. They have, or believe they have, an immediate call to their work that comes from the divine power that rules the stars in their courses. That call was experienced with some degree of social dislocation. It disrupted personal ties, social scripts, and well-worn identities. So be it! These persons paid the price and followed that call. If they experience a season of vocational doubt later on, as most church leaders do, it registers first as a strain in the relationship with the One who called them to the work. God, did I mishear your call? Lord, was I only imaging your summons?

And for every immediate call to ministry there is also what the church calls the "mediated call," the validation of the individual's call by the larger church.[6] Not everyone hearing voices out there is hearing the voice of the Lord calling them to ministry! And so the church appoints gatekeepers and these gatekeepers enter into a covenant of mutual discernment with persons who believe they have heard the call. Interviews will be held. Tests will be taken and retaken. Mentors will be assigned. These days the length and comprehensiveness of the discernment process may tax the tenacity of even the most resolute souls. But those who endure the process win the prize: the *public* validation of what may have been a very private and eccentric call. And that can be a great source of confidence. The church leader now carries a *recognition* that sustains against seasons of private doubt. There are significant others who see him or her as indeed called by God. From time to time the people of God and the connection of colleagues may point the way forward with a nudge to "remember your call."

Church leaders also have *the power of holding a public office that inspires projections of benevolence, knowledge, and hope*. There is no dominant name for set-apart ministry across the centuries, only a variety of names. Some of them obviously reflect in-house theological concerns: overseer, priest, pastor, preacher, shepherd, and spiritual guide. Others are weighted toward the church's conversation with the surrounding culture: clergy, reverend, counselor, enabler, wounded healer, church leader, and coach.[7] All are labels projecting unalloyed esteem and trust. In practice that means church leaders have social capital from the moment they first enter into a relationship with a church community. They will be credited with skills and intelligence they may or may not have. They will be praised for enterprises where their involvement may have been either instrumental or marginal. They will be given the benefit of the doubt in disputes, at least for awhile.[8]

Church leaders continue to have *the power of being the resident theologian of the congregation*.[9] Constant reminders that the pastor is no longer the most educated member of the congregation seem hardly the point! The pastor still is normally the most educated and most up-to-date person in the texts of the tradition, the tools of the office, and the disciplines of formation. Those who challenge the necessity of a seminary education must develop elaborate schemes for sneaking in the back door the theological knowledge they throw out the front door.

Somebody has to be the most well-grounded and up-to-date theological voice in the congregation. Somebody needs to be able to respond when participants in the Jesus Seminar make reckless statements that grab the headlines of newspapers and magazines.

Somebody needs to describe why the church must care about inclusive language. Somebody must take the lead in those occasions when the questions concerning suffering and God hang heavy in the air. Someone must intervene when the worship team regresses from trinitarian orthodoxy. Church leaders equipped by education to be theologians are seasoned by encounter to become resident theologians. Through trial and error they secure a more confident voice for the teaching office, and with that voice, the respect of the people.

Church leaders have *the power of Spirit endowment*. There are moments when church leaders are borne aloft, performing better than their accrued skills. It is *given them* to say the right word at a hospital bed, to interrupt the order of worship, to approach a certain potential donor. In the best tradition of the Bible's teaching on the Spirit's yoked visitation, a teaching evident in 1 and 2 Samuel, the Spirit both elevates the leader and prepares the hearts of the people to receive his or her leadership. A one-sided emphasis on the leader's charismatic gifts misses the fullness of event.[10] The Spirit is experienced as an energy field arching over the challenge of the moment, the people of God, and the leader God summons to that confluence. Leaders who have been instruments of the Spirit's timely use often experience an "afterglow" as they labor in the midst of the congregation. It is a form of power, potent and potentially dangerous both to them and to the congregation they serve.[11]

Church leaders also have the more everyday *power that accrues from successful reflective practice*. They are like architects holding together the principles of geometry and the eccentricities of environment. They are like psychotherapists borrowing eclectically from schools of thought to help a patient. The church leader stands at the intersection of knowledge and experience, not entirely bound by either, but strongly committed to both.[12] Church leaders sustain in their person a convergence of the energy of the texts and the energy of fresh experience. The former gives them language for the occasion and the advantage of collective experience. The latter gives them the urgency of the occasion and the encounter with life's irreducible structure as story. And as church leaders make the right moves, as they lead worship with finesse, as they untangle the knots of dysfunctional groups, as they offer just the right words at the funeral of a suicide, they earn the "second ordination" of the congregation's respect.

Finally, church leaders have *the power of access*. In an age of professional distance on the one hand and personal cocooning on the other, church leaders retain a remarkable freedom of entry. They go into hospitals, homes, work situations, and the streets for the sake of taking their work to the people rather than waiting for the people to come to them. They have immediate access to persons when those persons are at their best and worst. They carry things said in confidence. They often see others with their social armor set aside. They have an unspoken permission to lance wounds for the sake of healing. They can force needed conversations. Church leaders know the vulnerabilities of the persons committed to their care.

Listening to Abigail

The church leader cast as the spear thrower rather than the one ducking them is so unpleasant an image that it invites denial. It is hard for church leaders to face the presence of anger, and it is difficult for them to avoid the subtle ways of acting it out in pious camouflage. It is harder yet for them to assess realistically their considerable power and the subtle ways that power can be used in the service of vengeance. There is praise withheld. There are occasions boycotted. There is the distancing from others in the time of their distress. There is subterfuge of a plan. There is malicious gossip. There are those in-your-face violations of ministerial etiquette. There are even brazen acts of immorality or illegality.

In the end there is a violence that can undo the kingdom, and that violence would have its way except for the presence of someone like an importunate woman named Abigail. She may appear today in the person of a spouse or confidant who helps us remember the specific unhappy episode we morphed into a fatalistic worldview. She may show up as a judicatory supervisor or colleague who candidly observes: "You came down a little heavy-handed on that one, didn't you?" Or sometimes our Abigail is what she is in 1 Samuel 25: a stranger who, in a timely way, manages to break the spell of our ire, sparing us the repercussions of a vengeful act, and keeping our hands clean for the consensus building work of church leadership.

CHAPTER SEVEN

DANCING MADLY

2 Samuel 6:12-23
David danced before the LORD with all his might. David
was girded with a linen ephod. (6:14a)

W e search for the secret of leadership like we search for the
secret of love, success, and other things that mean a lot to
us. We usually start our search, as have the majority of
students of leadership from ancient times to the present, by trying to
name some irreplaceable trait exhibited by persons who lead. In the
West this tradition has two origins. One source is certain passages of
the Hebrew Bible, such as Sirach 44–50 that starts out, "Let us now
sing the praises of famous men, our ancestors in their generations."[1]
The litany names persons and their qualities: Noah's faithfulness,
Joshua's courage, Solomon's wisdom, and so on. The other source is
Plutarch's *Parallel Lives* where fifty Greek leaders have their counterpart in fifty Roman leaders.[2] The preferred traits cataloged
now have a classic ring about them, things like: following the
dictates of justice, standing against the crowd, and facing danger
courageously.

The tradition of looking for the traits of effective leaders extends
through the Renaissance period when persons looked to the ancient
past for better patterns. One of the most enduring leadership books is
from that time: Machiavelli's *The Prince* (1513) replaces idealism with
hard political realism, but still basically paints a picture of an individual exercising timely skills. Regardless of circumstance, the leader
must know how to be assertive yet unassuming, diplomatic yet firm.[3]

Modern Europeans and Americans in turn looked to the Renaissance and the classics for their education in leadership. Thomas Carlyle transmits this tradition in *On Heroes, Hero-Worship, and the Heroic in History* (1840).[4] He says great leaders are endowed with certain traits with which they are able to capture the imagination of the masses and mobilize them for collective action. Great prophets like Muhammad, great poets like Dante, great "priests" like Luther and Knox have independence and "valor." They are passionate and energetic. They are what we would call the movers and shakers. They excel at motivation. William James agrees that the history of the world is basically the history of these Great Ones; they are the fundamental forces behind all social change.[5]

Leadership studies of the last century continue the quest to name the trait or virtue that explains effective leadership. Is the deciding factor appearance? Are leaders, for example, taller than most? (Not necessarily, but studies show physical stature can come into play.)[6] Are leaders more articulate, more ambitious, more self-assured than others? Is there something in their genetic code that determines they are "born to leadership"? Does birth order have something to do with it? When all is said and done should we measure leadership potential by intelligence? Or is emotional intelligence a better indicator? Some have found the key to the leader's effectiveness in attention to detail, others in the ability to stand back and see the big picture. Where do leaders emerge on the introvert-extrovert continuum? Is leadership a matter of vision and conviction or a matter of adapting to pressing forces? Some have seen the secret of leadership in ambition, others in persistence, still others in integrity.[7] One author only half-jokingly sees the secret of leadership in a healthy dose of paranoia.[8]

Church leaders draw upon these studies, usually second or third hand. We gather up the traits offered by these studies and freely project them into biblical texts and onto biblical characters like throwing darts at a stationary board. And yet church leaders often have vague second thoughts about the practice. We name this or that trait of leadership and even factor in the situation's influence on the moment of leadership, but it still feels like something is missing. How do you explain why one qualified person is available for the moment of leadership when other qualified persons are not? Do the biblical texts themselves introduce any unique factor into the debate? It just feels like they should and that our search is unfinished until we find that factor.

It is the witness of 1 and 2 Samuel that the secret of leadership is a robust intimacy with God. Traits and situations count, but they are not the overriding factor.

Listening to the Books of Samuel

No episode in the books of Samuel better captures the complexities of relationship between divine, personal, and public power than David's dancing before the ark in 2 Samuel 6:12-23. David's dancing is not a neutral act of praise. The ark, the symbol of the presence of God, is being transferred to Jerusalem, David's city. This represents a pivotal transfer of political power at the height of David's personal power as a leader. But it also represents a transforming possibility for a new understanding of leadership by subordinating personal and public power to God's power. The king is unashamedly stripped of royal vestments and unreservedly committed to abandoned dancing in devotion to the God whose power makes all human power possible.

Of course, David has been charged in this episode with cynical manipulation of religious symbols (the ark) for the sake of his own enhanced power. His capital now becomes the religious center of Israel. Michal, Saul's daughter, scorns him for "uncovering himself . . . shamelessly" (v. 20), and David's reply that he will "make myself yet more contemptible than this" (v. 22) signals the end of the house of Saul through the notice (v. 23) that Michal was given no child (by David or by God?).

Is David's robust intimacy with God, seen in this dance, a genuine recognition and honoring of divine power as the source of true leadership or a cynical use of religious symbol to consolidate personal power? Perhaps this account invites us to reflect on how thin the line is between these two possibilities and how constantly leadership in ministry must struggle to avoid crossing that line.

This moment does not come isolated from the rest of David's story. David, like all leaders of God's people, begins his leadership journey with a sense of God's call. It then makes sense that a leadership that begins with God's call must be constantly measured by evidence of an ongoing and intimate relationship with God.

We have seen in earlier chapters that Saul began with many of the same promising traits that marked David with leadership potential. Both were tall, popular, courageous, skilled in battle, and anointed by the prophet Samuel as a sign of God's calling. Yet, Saul was constantly falling out of connection with God. He is fearful when he should be trusting, cautious when he should be bold, and envious when he should be welcoming. The difference comes when Saul forgets that he has resources for leadership that lie beyond himself and center in the God who called him. In the end, Saul turns a violent hand against God's priests (1 Sam. 22) and himself (1 Sam. 31).

By contrast, David seems constantly to be engaged in prayer and praise. He has wonderful personal traits and gifts, but he refuses to rely on his own traits alone. He faces Goliath but only after prayer. He includes two priests (Abiathar and Zadok) in his closest circle even while running from Saul in the wilderness. He prays so often that his men sometimes grow impatient. He refuses to raise his hand against Saul, who is trying to kill him, out of respect for God's anointed (1 Sam. 24 and 26). David is the "man after God's own heart" (1 Sam. 13:14), and the text repeatedly says that "the LORD was with him" (1 Sam. 16:18b; 17:37; 18:12, 14, 28; 20:13; 2 Sam. 5:10). David's trust in the Lord is such that he boldly takes actions that break the rules when he is convinced of the direction God would have him take. He requests and receives the holy bread of the priests when his men are famished and on the run (1 Sam. 21) and takes refuge with the Philistines, Israel's traditional enemy (1 Sam. 27). The bringing of the ark back to a place of honor is itself a bold move. David's story up to the point of his dancing is one marked by many evidences of the active presence of God. It is not accidental that tradition attributes much of the prayers and praises of the Psalms to David.

Thus, when David dances before the ark, the reader of his story already has some evidence that this is more than a cynical and self-serving act. It is entirely consistent with David's story to see in his unashamed celebration an expression of a robust intimacy with God that was at the center of his leadership.

Indeed, as David's story continues, it is when he loses touch with that intimate relationship with God and trusts in his own authority and power that he gets into serious trouble. In later chapters we will deal with these sad and tragic episodes in the story of David's leadership of God's people. There have unfortunately been many leaders in the community of God's people who have confused success with faithfulness. David was at the height of his success when his loss of being centered in God's presence brought his kingdom and his family to tragedy.

David is a leader called by God who saw clearly that his leadership centered in an unreserved openness to God's presence and power in his life. His many fine qualities might have made him a leader anyway. The events of his day may have given him the opportunity to have an impact. But it was only the presence of God that could make his leadership faithful to the high purposes for which God had called him.

In dancing before the ark David became a political leader who dared to become involved in the religious life of his people. Pastoral leaders today may face the opposite challenge, to be religious leaders who risk involvement in the public issues of our time. Yet, the issue is the same at root. Leadership in the service of the God who calls men and women to serve God's people must be carried out in recognition that God cares for and reigns over all of life, in all of its aspects. There is no leadership committed to intimate relationship with God that can be compartmentalized and limited to the realms of our comfort zones. God calls us to put off the robes of our comfortable roles and dance into risky futures as leaders who do not manage God but serve God.

Second Samuel 6 contains a reminder in verses 6-8 that leadership lived in intimacy with God is not just pragmatic career development but risky business. It is the story of the death of Uzzah. It is an unwelcome reminder that the holiness of God is dangerous if taken lightly.

We know nothing about Uzzah. We do know that the ark was, by law, to be carried on poles by Levites, but it has instead been loaded on an oxcart. Was Uzzah responsible for this? Is his haste to prevent the toppling of the ark in reality his own attempt to avoid the consequences of poor judgment in transporting the holy presence? As a priest, did he not know that touching the ark is forbidden? Such questions cannot be answered, but the death of Uzzah can stand as a reminder of the danger of trying to manage God's holiness. What should be reverence and awe before God gives way to the notion that we can put our hands on God. That way leads to death—perhaps not as dramatic as Uzzah's, but just as fatal. Jesus called those who thought they could control God's holiness by their own efforts "whitewashed tombs . . . full of dead man's bones" (Matt. 23:27).

Between the disregard of God's holiness by Saul and the control of God's holiness by Uzzah lies David's dance. David models a leadership that stands before God without the trappings of human authority, without reservation, without pretension. David does not cease to be the person of courage, judgment, and diplomacy we have seen in the earlier stories of his life. The moment in Israel's life is certainly crucial and promising. But in David's dance both person and moment are submitted to the "practice of the presence of God"—a reminder to us of an intimacy with God which stands at the center of leadership in the church and constantly relates our practice to our calling.

A Robust Intimacy with God

To our list of respectable leadership profiles dare we add these: a leader who dances before the Lord with all his might in the public square in an act of shameless abandon; a leader who has and will make good on his promise to be "yet more contemptible than this," now acting demented to avoid capture, now feeding his troops with the holy bread from the Tabernacle (1 Sam. 21); a leader who weeps and walks barefoot in the dust as an exiled king (2 Sam. 15); a leader who by the power of God "leaps over walls" (2 Sam. 22) and seems capable of surprising moves and sudden course corrections even into old age (2 Sam. 24)? The Bible calls David a leader "after God's own heart" (1 Sam. 13:14), but can we resonate with this passionate oh-so-human king whose robust intimacy with God gives his leadership a certain edge and edginess?

Actually, in recent years both secular and church leadership studies have given considerable attention to the subject of leaders' need to provide some distance between themselves and the immediacy of their situations. Three particular models seem to endure in one form or another.

The self-differentiated leader of family systems thought. This leader's autonomy is expressed in terms of mature membership in a healthy family system. "Differentiation means the capacity of a family member to define his or her own life's goals and values apart from surrounding togetherness pressures, to say 'I' when others are demanding 'you' and 'we.' "[9] The premise is that a church or synagogue acts so much like a family system in its emotional intensity that the application of family systems studies to the life of the congregation will yield rich insights on the nature of congregational leadership. Differentiated leaders are set in contrast to leaders who surrender to various games of unhealthy congregational family systems. They are not pulled into a congregation's skewed lines of communication (secrets). They refuse to enter into family feuds where those who offer the invitation have no intention of changing (triangulation). They resist the congregation's attempts to misdirect blame (scapegoating). They are immune to the congregation's chronic anxiety; they are a nonanxious presence.

The self-aware leader of emotional intelligence thought. From the seventies a number of persons have argued for supplementing or even replacing the standard intelligence quotient (IQ) approach to potential for leadership. Specifically they want to find a more accurate way to measure the relational skills that are at the heart of successful leadership.[10] Does the leader discern the morale of the people or is he or she too self-absorbed (emotional illiteracy)? Will the leader channel anger into constructive action or "lose it" (emotional hijacking) and thus also lose credibility? Persons give evidence of their emotional intelligence in the social arena with such skills as accurate empathy, reading the climate of an organization, motivating others, communicating effectively, and negotiating conflict. Those skills are layered upon another set closer to home. Emotionally intelligent leaders have an awareness of their feelings and the influence of those feelings on their ability to interpret and decide. They are able to manage disruptive emotions. They can adapt to change.[11] They are "in" but not "of" their work setting.

The "on the balcony" leader of reflective practitioner thought.
If leadership is about helping a group name and address its adaptive task then leadership is a matter of "reflection-in-action."[12] Effective leaders don't import their agenda or impose their direction. They take their cues from the evolving situation. They have a general acquaintance with a number of disciplines and schools of thought, but they are not sworn disciples to any of them. Instead they are creatively eclectic in their choice of tools and moves based on their reading of the situation. Like an experienced psychotherapist with a patient, or a town planner with an overtaxed environment, the leader alternately moves in close to learn and act, then backs up to digest and revise assumptions, then moves in close for more learning and action. While the primary focus is always outward, and the knowledge to be mastered is never far removed from the immediate situation, there must be times when leaders step back. Those who dance best on the floor cherish occasions for "getting on the balcony."

Church leaders have much to gain by applying these models to their practice, especially at a time when congregations react to real or perceived institutional decline by raising the bar of leadership expectations. But there is something still missing. David has the ability to step back from the immediacy of the situation, but that alone does not account for his effectiveness. For David, *the turning from the people of God is also a turning to the God of the people*. It is in the persistent and animated verbal intercourse with God that David finds the inspirations and the interludes he needs to be a leader after God's own heart.

The former shepherd from the fields near Bethlehem cannot talk about God (theology) very long before he slides into talk with God (doxology). "*The Lord* is my shepherd . . . *he* makes me lie down . . . *he* leads me beside still waters . . . *he* leads me in right paths . . . *you* are with me . . . *you* prepare a table before me . . . *you* anoint my head with oil" (Psalm 23, italics added). One commentator describes the combination of vulnerability and absolute trust in God as a "child at home." [13]

The commander of troops about to go out to battle rehearses his moves before God. *Will Saul try to destroy us?* He will. *Can the citizens of Keilah be trusted to shelter us?* They can't. *Dare we stay in this place or keep moving?* Keep moving (1 Sam. 23). Even when King David, at the height of his power, sins and suffers the consequences of his acts, the ruptured conversation is paramount. "Against you, you alone, have I sinned, and done what is evil in your sight" (Ps. 51:4).

Secular models of leaders stepping back from the overwhelming immediacy of their situations to gain perspective, as helpful as they may be, stop short of this animated conversation of leader and God. There is power in such disciplines of transcending reflection. But it is not the release that comes from pouring out heart and soul to God, what the theologian Pannenberg analyzes as a spontaneous soliloquy flowing from primal trust and love.[14] Nor is it the lift that comes from receiving timely messages of succor and direction from God.

Managers, Leaders, and Shame

Over the past seventy years an extensive secular literature has developed that compares and contrasts managing and leading.[15] Good managers lead and good leaders manage, and many of the skills that make for their respective effectiveness overlap. Both managers and leaders need relational abilities, learning skills, and the capacity to adapt. Secular leadership studies are not as quick as church leadership studies to jump to dramatic contrasts between the work of being an administrator and the work of being an executive. They are not as likely to vilify managers or idolize leaders when analyzing dysfunctional corporate cultures.[16] They are more prone to blended descriptions like "leader-manager" and more likely to locate those persons in a complex continuum of roles, activities, and behaviors.[17]

Still, there are bridges along the road of that continuum that "managers" must become "leaders" to cross. The literature tries to describe the differences between persons who can or can't cross those bridges. Perhaps it is a matter of temperament—leaders more solitary, charismatic, and driven; managers more social, tranquil, and pragmatic. Perhaps it is an intellectual bent—leaders more abstract and intuitive, managers more empirical and rational. Or maybe the difference is in attention, leaders preferring to focus on the boundary issues of an organization, managers on the linchpin issues.

The books of Samuel add a different, uniquely theological perspective to crossing the bridge from managing to leading. David, the man of robust intimacy with God, the man whose operational style is a spontaneous soliloquy flowing from primal trust and love, is also the man who challenges the weight of social tradition and taboo, the man who rises above shame. David dances before the Lord and the gathered people with all his might. Stripped down to a linen ephod, he rolls back his head in ecstasy, waves his arms heavenward, runs, leaps, and kicks up his heels. Neither external nor internal voices of shame sway him. He hears scornful words like, "How the king of Israel honored himself today . . . as any vulgar fellow might," but they do not reach the center from which he acts. In a crowd or all alone David performs for an audience of One.

Shame is not guilt, but in the church we have a tendency to confuse the two.[18] Guilt is the uncomfortable feeling that comes from doing something we agree is wrong. We feel remorse for causing an accident by driving too fast for the conditions or for failing to stay in touch with a friend recently widowed. We *should* feel remorse! Because we experience guilt regularly, we regularly need confession, fresh reminders of God's "yes" in spite of our sins, and support for our growth in virtues.

Shame is more primitive, irrational, and complex than guilt. Shame is "a family of meanings and phenomena, not a single experience or definition."[19] This family includes such members as feeling demeaned, feeling inferior, feeling acutely self-conscious, feeling depleted, feeling embarrassed, feeling put on display, feeling disgraced, feeling cut down, feeling that there's nowhere to hide but wanting to hide desperately. The common elements in these experiences are a sense of uncontrollable exposure, a sense of being looked at by critical others, and a sense of the self as helpless object rather than as responsible subject.[20]

Set aside for the moment whatever constructive purpose shame ultimately may serve for the individual.[21] Allow for the fact that there is a chronic shame that is pathology; persons suffering from it deserve compassion and treatment. There is still a large body of "normal" shame operating in our life together in institutions, including the institution of the church. It is a silent but strong means of social control.

There are local church power arrangements vested with an aura of sanctity. To challenge them would feel like committing a sacrilege. The pastor who questions the church's lax fiscal accountability procedures may end up feeling like a heretic or a villain. Is it worth it? There are denominational structures that once embodied the energy of vision and the integrity of mission, but now are dated and counterproductive. Yet they carry the numinous sanctity of a taboo, especially for those church leaders acculturated into the denomination's ethos over prolonged periods. The person who introduces a measure of reform at a judicatory session, perhaps a motion to transfer some arena of decision making to a different level, may suddenly be labeled as a "radical" and ostracized by colleagues. Why bother?

Persons who would lead, not just manage, the people of God must face the demons of shame that sometimes block the path of liberating truth and innovative action. They must wrestle those demons in the frowns of faces gathered round the table, in the averted eyes of disapproving supervisors, and often in the haunts of their own restless dreams at 3:00 A.M.

Facing such shame head-on is a more difficult way to exercise a calling. But God can do things with David that God cannot do with his more domesticated contemporaries. The clue is in the dancing madly. God can do things with a person who rises above the fear of "uncontrollable exposure, a sense of being looked at by critical others" that God can never do with a person holding back for fear of being shamed. A church leader abandoned to "my God, my rock, in whom I take refuge" (2 Sam. 22:3) is less predictable but more effective than one who is always looking around to see if *they* give their blessing.

CHAPTER EIGHT

INFIDELITY

2 Samuel 11:1–12:15

In the spring of the year, the time when kings go out to battle, David sent Joab with his officers and all Israel with him. . . . But David remained at Jerusalem. (11:1)

Churches are charged environments where persons follow restless hearts, question their loyalties, and dream dreams of fulfillment.

Mandy is tired of the immature boys she dates at college: their insensitive comments, their lack of manners, their obsession with weekend sports and drinking. She wants long talks about deep things. She wants to throw her unbounded energy into the world's great problems. She hungers for adult recognition. With words from the poet Yeats she learned in English Literature (101), she longs for someone to "love the pilgrim soul" in her.

Catherine is still in shock over the desertion by the husband who left her and their five children (the oldest fourteen) for a younger woman with a better figure and freer lifestyle. Catherine's self-esteem is practically nonexistent these days. She operates in over-drive, pushing and pulling the children through the day, then collapses in exhaustion at night. She has no wish to return to the way it was; their marriage was never that good. But she does wish she could break the long spell of depression that drains color from even the brightest moments. She needs a way forward.

Jim is feeling his age (fifty-nine years) and the loss of time and opportunities. His feet are swollen at the end of the day. His doctor forbids almost everything he would like to eat or drink. He has reached a plateau at work and keeps hearing rumors about a major cutback. How could he start over at sixty? His wife is absorbed in her own disappointments; his grown children do not seem to need him as much as they once did. Some evenings Jim imagines himself walking out the back door, following the sun into the west, and never looking back.

Whether out of habit or chance, Mandy, Catherine, and Jim show up at church. They have come to the right place. Here people revel in the language of risk and confidence. Here people brandish heady labels like "friend of God" and lofty reputations like "spiritually gifted." Here people name the darker sides of life and also the powers by which they may be overcome or endured. And here in the center of this forward-looking movement, the people of God who stretch out to meet the future reign of God are the church leaders specifically called by God to authenticate the message of hope and safeguard the integrity of the enterprise.

Church leaders show up at the church with personal agendas too. They have needs, hungers, and fantasies. Their marriages are more or less solvent. Church leaders are adrift in complex life passages that amplify their sense of frailty, injury, and the shortness of time.[1] They need the same things they are there to offer others: the vision of larger purposes, the honesty to face personal demons, the hope that overcomes the vagaries of despair.

Church leaders may possess this vision, honesty, and hope. Or, in an atmosphere where the line between spiritual intimacy and sexual intimacy is very thin,[2] church leaders may grow careless. They may run from their call, abuse the considerable power that accrues to their office, and initiate or allow themselves to be lured into tawdry liaisons that end in pain, disgrace, and even loss of ministerial office.

If the other person in those liaisons happens to be vulnerable like Mandy, Catherine, or Jim, chances are that person will end up a cipher in the stories that follow just as Bathsheba does in the story of David's infidelity. Their pain, disgrace, and loss is no less real than that of the leaders, but they lack the protection of professional rank, the advantage of a public voice, and the cloak of sanctity.[3]

Listening to the Books of Samuel

In 2 Samuel 11–12 David's story takes a dramatic turn. The shift has been described in a variety of ways, but they all signal a change for the worse in David's character, his future, and his relationship with God. The shift can be seen as the movement from a story of blessing to a story of curse, or perhaps as a turning from gift to grasp. David's attitude moves from one of grateful receiving of God's gifts to self-centered grasping by his own power. By the end of these chapters, David's world is transformed. Nothing will be the same. David uses the leadership power of his office as king of God's people to satisfy his own personal desires. Moreover, the violent use of power he had earlier avoided (see chapter 6, 1 Sam. 24–26) now spirals out of control in his life. The violence that stains David's hands will spread to his own family (2 Sam. 12–19) and will endanger the people David leads.

The story may be seen as a tale of royal power in four episodes, each with a complication that further enmeshes David in sin:

Prologue (v. 1). An introductory verse places David at home while his army lays siege to Rabbah. David is not exercising the leadership for which he was known. Perhaps he is weary of his role or he may feel less effective than he once did. Whatever the reason, the mood has shifted in David's story from the vigor of leadership to brooding over personal needs.

(1) The Adultery (vv. 2-5). David sees a beautiful woman (Bathsheba) bathing and exercises royal privilege to "take" her (v. 4). He uses the power of his leadership role in a coercive way that fulfills the warning of the prophet Samuel (1 Sam. 8:11-18) that kings often "take" what they desire from the people they lead. Both the NIV and NRSV soften this verb by relating that David sends messengers to "get" her. Taking is reduced to fetching, and the subject of the verb is changed from David to the messengers. But relationships that involve the power of a king are not romances between equals, and "take" is the actual verb used in the Hebrew account.

Complication: Bathsheba becomes pregnant.

(2) The Cover-up (vv. 6-13). David brings Uriah, Bathsheba's husband, home from the battlefront to sleep with his wife and remove suspicions over the child's paternity. Threatened with

exposure, David has no desire for continuing the relationship with Bathsheba.

Complication: Uriah is too dedicated as a soldier and will not "go down" to his house while his comrades are still in the field.

(3) The Murder (vv. 14-25). David arranges with Joab for Uriah to die in battle. David's initial misuse of power now escalates into a further abuse of his role as leader. He uses his position as commander-in-chief to order a murder. The abuse of leadership power will spiral out of control when self-interest prevails over the good of the community.

Complication: Other innocent lives are lost in an ill-advised military tactic.

(4) The Aftermath (vv. 26-27). David and Bathsheba marry to preserve public honor, and a son is born. If leadership of the people of God were only a human enterprise—a job—then David might escape accountability for his actions. Evil is not always caught and punished in the human world. But David's leadership arises out of the call of God to serve God's people. It is a vocation, and accountability is not simply measured in human terms.

Complication: David's actions were "evil in the sight of the LORD" (v. 11:27*b* [NASB]).

This final sentence of chapter 11 points beyond the boundaries of the story. In the books of Samuel the story is not just about the rise of royal power in Israel. It is also the story of God's power as the true force shaping Israel's future. Chapter 11 as only a story of David the king would have meant that the marriage and birth were the end of the matter. But as a story of God's anointed one, the matter is not ended. The story continues in chapter 12 where Nathan the prophet confronts David and announces divine judgment on David's actions in taking Bathsheba and killing Uriah. We will return to this prophetic encounter in a moment.

David's adultery with Bathsheba and the murder of Uriah is a classic story of the arrogant misuse of power for personal whim. It is remarkable that a story so negative to David was preserved and passed on in the tradition. Indeed the idealized Davidic portrait by the Chronicler omits this episode. We should be grateful that those who transmitted the tradition had the courage to present Israel's greatest king with a portrait that includes his weaknesses and vulnerability as well as his accomplishments and power. This sordid and disillusioning episode in David's story serves as a cautionary tale on the proximity of violence to those who live with power and of the temptations that are a part of every significant leadership role. It reminds us that those who are most admired and most accomplished are not immune to the temptation of power.

Those possessed of power and surrounded by admirers and supporters often succumb to the illusion that they are in control of their own destiny and can define the terms of the morality that governs their actions. David, however, experienced the limits of his power and control. He could not control Bathsheba's pregnancy, Uriah's principles, or God's moral judgment. One can hardly consider this a word limited in application to an ancient king when our own news has been filled in recent years with stories of politicians, clergy, military officers, and teachers guilty of sexual misconduct and self-interested manipulation of others. In many of these instances abuses were committed under the illusion that the authority of their office, rank, or influence would provide protection. The tragedy of lives undone and accomplishments overshadowed by such acts is an almost weekly story in our communities and nation.

The story of David's adultery and murder reminds us of the deadly spiral of violence that can escalate from a single act of sin. For David such an act born of lust led to an elaborate and deceitful attempt at cover-up, and finally to murder. Perhaps the dramas of our lives are not on this grand scale, but we should not imagine that this is not our story. We all know that we have acted at times to exploit others for our own self-interest, and we know too well how easily a lie to cover our tracks can involve us in complex deceits and additional acts that compound and deepen our original complicity.

Evidence that this story strikes close to home can be seen in the many efforts to soften the impact of the story. This is apparent in the endless fascination with the tale of David and Bathsheba through the generations and the many efforts to find some justification or mitigating circumstances that avoid the simple conclusion that David, the hero of our story, has become an adulterer and a murderer. These efforts are seen not only in scholarly treatments, from the ancient rabbis to modern academics, but in numerous treatments of the David and Bathsheba story in art, poetry, literature, and film.

As modern readers, teachers, and preachers we must face the harsh realities of the story and avoid the temptation to soften them. To do so will mean countering many distorted readings of this story already present in interpretation and popular culture. These distorted readings take several forms:

Scapegoating. Perhaps the most common distortion of this story through the ages is the effort to portray Bathsheba as a seductress or coconspirator, thereby transforming David, to some degree, from perpetrator to victim. The story gives us nothing explicit to substantiate such views and, in fact, shows little interest in Bathsheba as a subject at all. These efforts to make Bathsheba the initiator are unfortunately consistent with a common defense in cases of rape and abuse, that the victim "asked for it." Even the NRSV and NIV softening of the verb "take," with David as subject, to merely "get," with the messengers as subject (v. 4a), shows our unwillingness to face the coercion in David's action. This suggests the difficulty in facing similarly coercive behaviors between the sexes in our own experience. Indeed, when beloved leaders, including pastors, are exposed in misuses of power for sexual purposes it is often the partner who is blamed as initiator or seducer. Such persons, victimized by a powerful leader, are victimized again by public opinion.

Rationalizing. Another common effort to soften the harsh realities of this story is the search for mitigating circumstances that help explain if not justify David's actions. In a 1985 film, *King David*, Bathsheba reveals to a shocked David that Uriah is an abusive husband, thus giving David a noble motive for the act of murder and the rescue of an abused woman. The ancient rabbis likewise sought to lessen David's guilt in a variety of ways. Some claimed the chain of events was due to the marriage of a Hittite to an Israelite wife and that the subsequent marriage to David rectified that unacceptable state.

Leaders in the role of caregivers to their people often easily rationalize improper relationships as caring acts. But David's story forces us to see such situations for what they are—misuses of power by the one in the role of leader.

Romanticizing. A recent student paper described Bathsheba as the beautiful woman with whom "David fell in love when he saw her bathing." What better way to soften the harshness of this story than to make it a love story. Indeed, David and Bathsheba often make the list of history's great lovers alongside Romeo and Juliet, Antony and Cleopatra, and others. Hollywood could not resist this temptation and many people's view of this story is colored by the sweeping romance of Gregory Peck and Susan Hayward in Darryl F. Zanuck's 1951 film, *David and Bathsheba*. This film presents Uriah as a soldier with no interest in his wife, David as lonely in his royal office, and Bathsheba as a neglected wife who finds her true love in David. But the biblical text does not give us a romance. David has no interest in ongoing relationship or marriage until Bathsheba becomes pregnant, and even then he prefers the solution of making Uriah the father. Romances do not begin with "taking" and end with murder. We romanticize this tale at our own peril. Leaders, like all persons, may have unhappy marriages and troubled lives. A new relationship appears as romantic and renewing as one ignores the coercive power that seldom allows such relationships to be genuine or romantic for long.

When we preach and teach this story we must be clear. It is a story of a fallen hero. One cannot help recalling David's own lament over Saul and Jonathan, "How the mighty have fallen" (2 Sam. 1:19). This time it is David who has fallen, and the fall is not in battle but in moral character. The harsh reality of this story and the difficulty we have facing it is a testimony to the ease with which we excuse our own sin. But if we can acknowledge David's sin, we may better face our own sin as David does when confronted by Nathan in 2 Samuel 12.

To preach this story will require us to honestly admit our own complicity with David. To face the sin of our greatest biblical heroes can allow us to confess our own impulses to use others for the fulfillment of our own desires. It can force us to acknowledge the tragic ease with which we can become entangled in growing webs of sinful acts as we try to cover up and avoid accountability for our own manipulation of others. This story is especially directed to those whose positions of power, leadership, and influence provide constant opportunity for manipulation or exploitation of vulnerable others. Our news stories are filled with stories of people—from Presidents to pastors—who have abused the power of their offices for the fulfillment of their own self-interested desires or gains. We need to preach this bleak side of David's story, not simply to address the sins of the powerful, but to acknowledge how often we excuse and emulate them.

In 2 Samuel 11:4 David "sent" in order to "take." In 2 Samuel 12:1 the Lord "sent" the prophet Nathan in order to "speak." Nathan is to confront David and speak God's judgment that what David has done is "evil in the sight of the LORD" (11:27b [NASB]).

Nathan tells David a story about an abuse of power committed by a wealthy man and David quickly pronounces judgment on such arrogance. Nathan reveals that the story is a parable for David's own action, "You are the man!" (12:7) and pronounces an oracle of judgment. This chapter is not the place to focus on the task of prophetic speaking in leadership. Certainly elsewhere we would emphasize such boldness. His prophetic speaking to power is itself an act of leadership worthy of consideration.

But here we would emphasize an aspect of this episode of confrontation often overlooked. *Both* Nathan and David stand within and represent the community of faith and the future of God's people. God's people cannot afford to read this story simply as a call to become Nathan, pointing fingers at and naming the sins of others. Seldom are the leaders in the community of faith either wholly righteous or unredeemably wicked. There is, of course, a role in leadership for those willing to speak truth to power, to be Nathan when God calls us to take that risk. But the emphasis here is on our ability to stand in David's role and acknowledge the difficult word we sometimes need to hear, "You are the one!"

The story of 2 Samuel 12 focuses primarily on the speaking of judgment, but it also speaks of the possibilities of confession and repentance in the face of judgment.

David's immediate and direct confession of sin (v. 13a) is almost as surprising as Nathan's climactic "You are the man!" (v. 7a). David's crimes lead to brokenness, and consequences unfold from this brokenness. They will unfold in the death of the child and the further tragedies that will infect David's family. David has loosed the power of death, but with his confession of guilt he reclaims the possibilities of life in the midst of death. He is brought from his own self-pronounced verdict that he is a "son of death" (v. 5b) to Nathan's quiet word, "You will not die" (v. 13b).

If, as leaders of God's people, we attend only to Nathan's judgment and fail to note David's repentance, then we run the risk of settling for guilt as the goal of our prophetic speech to others or the final truth about our own lives. The good news of this text is that we are not left in guilt but are called to repentance and are forgiven. This does not mean we escape consequences for our sin. David's self-centered abuses of power will return to haunt him through his own children. But judgment is not the final word; repentance makes a word of life possible in the face of that judgment. As the church speaks the truth to power, it should never hold the self-satisfied assumption that judgment is the final word. The word of judgment must contain the hope that confession and repentance make life possible in spite of the deathly powers unleashed by sin.

Reading this story as our own story in both the roles of Nathan and David may allow for the possibility that as leaders we might speak and hear this word of truth to ourselves. If we are forced to hear and face our own complicity in self-interested abuses of power through the confrontations of Nathan, then also we, like David, may be able to confess, repent, and take a new direction away from such abuses. Reading such stories this way may encourage us to avoid or abandon paths of temptation and deceit.

In many medieval synagogue manuscripts of this chapter, a gap was left by the copyist in the text following David's confession of sin in verse 13*a*. This gave the opportunity for the reading of Psalm 51, the great penitential psalm that carries the superscription: "A Psalm of David, when the prophet Nathan came to him, after he had gone in to Bathsheba." This psalm expresses the attitude of repentance the church seeks when it speaks in judgment:

> Have mercy on me, O God,
>   according to your steadfast love;
> according to your abundant mercy
>   blot out my transgressions.
> Wash me thoroughly from my iniquity,
>   and cleanse me from my sin. . . .
>
> Create in me a clean heart, O God,
>   and put a new and right spirit within me.
> Do not cast me away from your presence,
>   and do not take your holy spirit from me.

> Psalm 51:1-2; 10-11

AWOL

Second Samuel hints at a story it does not tell: the story of David's withdrawal from his public destiny. The man who was supposed to be the people's king, the one who would "go out before us and fight our battles" (1 Sam. 8:20), instead sends out the troops and stays behind in Jerusalem where he becomes fascinated with the wife of one of his field commanders.

The siren calls of romantic fantasies and sexual temptations fill the air the church leader breathes. There are victims of spousal neglect who are overly responsive to the leader's smallest move of kindness or attention. There are desperate seekers for love and affirmation appearing on the radar screen of the leader's instincts for compassion and rescue. There are church "groupies" blossoming in the charged atmosphere of religious theater where the church leader is vested with colorful distinction and stars in public performance. These persons can break down the resistance of the strongest church leader in the most confident phase of his or her calling. For the leader who struggles with questions of identity or esteem, these persons may be especially attractive. There is a point in every temptation when the church leader's only recourse for resisting the siren calls that lead to destruction is to request help from colleagues. The image of Odysseus bound *by others* to the mast of the ship with ears plugged with wax against the siren calls is still appropriate.[4] But before that moment of crisis arrives there are other moments when choice is more clearly an option. Like David before the Bathsheba episode, church leaders can decide whether or not to remain back in Jerusalem while the troops go out to battle. Church leaders can decide whether to stay engaged in the drama of the congregation's story and its struggle to face adaptive issues or to continue to drift toward disengagement. They can choose to sustain collegial connections where they receive the reality check that comes from being around others who are "yet alive"[5] after following God's call to ministry through thick and thin, or they can opt out of those connections. Church leaders can remain accountable to mentors and spiritual guides they trust "to smite gently" (John Wesley) with words of truth in love, or they can choose to let such commitments slide.

Closer to home, church leaders can choose to ignore stress symptoms in their marriages: the once strident exchanges that have turned to sullen avoidance of the subject, the physical and emotional inhibitors of sexual intimacy that go unquestioned, and the quiet loss of resonance for each other's unfolding providence.

Closest to home of all, church leaders can choose to ignore the loss of robust intimacy with God. The drifting that follows from that loss is dangerous territory. Reclaiming the primal trust and conversation is the first step to becoming connected again, and reconnecting to God is the best immunization against the darker side of romantic fantasies and sexual temptations. Church leaders need not encounter the power of sexual passions armed only with will and intellect; they may encounter them armed with the strength of an even greater passion.

Power and Sex

Forsaking his public call and destiny David sends for Bathsheba. The commentary points out that a long history of scapegoating, rationalizing, and romanticizing has accumulated around the story of David and Bathsheba.[6] The bottom line remains that it is an act of coercive sex. With the advantage of superior power and driven by lust, David takes Bathsheba. He takes her as brazenly as the rich man in Nathan's parable takes the poor man's pet ewe lamb to feed a guest.

The manifold power that makes church leaders dangerous when they are angry also makes them dangerous when they are engaged in romantic projections and sexual escapades with church members or with others who seek their help. The work of Marie Fortune and others has raised the level of the public discourse concerning this issue.[7] Today the censure surrounding an exposed or confessed incident of clergy infidelity in the parish will normally include the charge of abuse of the power of that office. Today Bathsheba has as much a chance of being construed a victim as a temptress—at least at the level of public discourse. But at the level of clergy self-awareness there is more work to be done as countless stories like the following make clear.

No one could believe John's brazenness. First he became roman-tically involved with Sally, a woman twenty years younger than he who had come to him as her pastor for help with an abusive hus-band. Next John placed her on the worship committee without con-sulting anyone. His deference to her eccentric suggestions was embarrassing to other members of the committee. "Counseling appointments" were routinely scheduled after evening meetings. John would say goodnight to others and promise to turn out the lights and lock up while Sally waited in front of his office. When Sally's old car broke down, John began to chauffeur her to the gro-cery store, to the doctor's office, even to Wal-Mart where parish-ioners would scramble in elaborate moves of avoidance. Finally John and Sally began to take long rides in the country "just to get away." One late afternoon a park ranger came upon them in a romantic embrace in a no trespassing section of the grounds surrounding the town reservoir. It was a small town; the ranger was a leader in John's congregation. In the ungracious days that followed, a long and bright pastoral career ended on a sour note, a troubled woman sank deeper into misery, a parsonage marriage in crisis held on by only a thin thread, and the soul of a congregation was stricken with anger and grief.

John's life was littered with issues of frustration. His marriage felt the strain of supporting an adult child who seemed incapable of independence. He suffered the slight of being passed over several times for judicatory positions in favor of persons who, at least in John's estimation, didn't come close to his qualifications for the work. The building committee at the church was indifferent to John's liturgically correct suggestions for sanctuary renovation. His associate pastor was a "prima donna" too busy with his own career trajectory to be of much practical help with the congregation.

The problem was one of focus. John had considerable power: the power of call and church validation, the power of charismatic gifts, the power of skilled reflective practice, and the power of a public office with trust. But instead of bringing that power to bear on a weighty agenda of important issues, John allowed it to wander aim-lessly, a free-floating energy looking for a home.

Choosing Nathan

The self-absorbed and solitary leader cut off from the information that could have averted disaster is a familiar figure in secular leadership studies. This figure appears across the entire spectrum of leadership settings. Commanders, lost in their private bravado, ignore battlefront reports and refuse counsel from officers. The classic twentieth-century example is Hitler in the last days of the Third Reich.[8] CEOs and CFOs are so busy raising investor confidence that they ignore structures of fiscal accountability, as with the recent investment scandals on Wall Street. Defeated and sulking politicians, even Presidents, surround themselves with adoring staff and flattering cronies rather than reach out to allies, face political problems head-on, and manage their hungers.[9]

Leadership studies of the last decade have used various names to describe and analyze the condition of the out-of-touch leader. Peter Drucker writes about the information-dependent climate of contemporary business and the dangers to leaders who ignore *information from outside*. Edgar Schein cautions against the leader in a corporate culture who is oblivious to *disconfirming data*. Daniel Goleman paints a grim picture of a leader in the public arena operating with deficient *social radar*.[10] Concerned judicatory leaders and colleagues in ministry resonate with the warnings of such studies with their constant reference to the specter of the Lone Ranger in the parish.

In ministry it is remarkably easy to become the commander who remains behind in Jerusalem while the troops go out to fight. The freedom from direct supervision can be the springboard for accrued virtue or vice. The nature of a volunteer organization can expand the leader's social skills or feed the leader's egocentric illusions. Church leaders may start out in ministry smarting from the gatekeepers' questions and the supervisor's stare, but eventually that all changes. Soon enough church leaders can find themselves in a rarefied atmosphere where "never is heard a discouraging word." In this atmosphere it is so easy to indulge in the white lies that become the entering wedge for larger lies. Those larger lies sap the energy needed for constructive action and soon have the power to place the veneer of social trust in jeopardy.[11] The downward spiral seen in the story of David and Bathsheba has a certain inescapable logic.

Enter Nathan. He is the one person who will stand up to David's power. As a prophet Nathan possesses the power to confront even a king with the truth. Nathan engages David in a story of a rich man's callous indifference and cruel actions as a way to mirror David's self-serving lies. The prophet helps the king to see how out of character he has been relative to his unfolding story from God.[12]

Like David, the church leader who flaunts power in callous acts of infidelity will be confronted one day. Someone will say "no": a judicatory supervisor, a local church personnel committee, a spouse, a lawyer for the wronged party, *someone!* But by then most of the damage has been done, and the repercussions of sin must be played out. The open question is whether church leaders can be deflected from near or early-course illicit affairs. Can anyone talk a church leader down from the ledge of a suicidal jump? Is there a Nathan among the friends and acquaintances of that church leader?

According to a long church tradition of pastoral practice there should be. In the act of giving corrective guidance or admonition (*admonitio*), the church leader fulfills a New Testament mandate for building up the people of God.[13] All Christians are expected to tell the truth in love, to participate in mutual correction. But church leaders have the added responsibility to do this as an expression of their care for the members of the corporate Body of Christ and of their commitment to word, order, and sacrament. It is a work of love as opposed to indifference to the sight of others in the state of danger. It is a discipline that requires courage, timing, and tact. It is a practice that strains the benevolent self-image of the one that admonishes and threatens the false hopes of the one admonished. Especially when the admonishing takes place between church leaders there is volatility in the air; the well-intended act can deteriorate in so many different directions. But admonition also can be the way out and the way back for the church leader overcome or nearly overcome by sin.

Most contemporary church leaders are not steeped in the tradition of mutual correction, and that should be no surprise. Today many of the classical church traditions of pastoral practice are dismissed or overlooked. When it comes to church leadership we prefer to look for water in other wells. This does not mean the practice of mutual correction is beyond our reach; it only means that there is no baseline of collegial experience or practice to lean upon in time of need. In our time the responsibility falls on the individual church leader to make a conscious decision to be vulnerable to corrective guidance from a colleague. We must choose our Nathans, and we must choose them before the time of testing.

On Not Shooting the Wounded

Whatever the present public climate for responding to a leader guilty of infidelity, whether more punitive or more forgiving, the Bible's primary story of such a leader unfolds in painful consequences but ends in restoration. A faithful general (Uriah) is the victim of a conspiracy and lies dead on the battlefield. The child born of the coercive union of David and Bathsheba dies. Seeds of political dissent are sown while the king neglects his office. The king's primal trust and conversation with God is lost. It will be a long road back, but it will be a road back, not a road to oblivion. The leader will stand before God again as a beloved asking, "What are you doing and where do I fit in?"

Metaphors from the church's tradition of mutual correction are sobering but ultimately hopeful. They receive their energy from actions like that of pulling weeds, threshing grain, and pruning the vine; or like that of taking bitter tonic, submitting to surgery, and breaking off an addiction. The ultimate purpose is restoration of the guilty party, just as pruning yields an abundant crop and surgery restores the patient's health.[14]

Weighty questions of supervisory responsibility and corporate liability must be asked. The victim's voice must be heard and restorative justice must be pursued. The church leader's story is no longer the only one that matters. That being agreed, the church leader's full story, the one that encompasses the theological foundations for his or her vocation also matter and must not be swept away with the repercussions of the sin.

Church leaders and church members must participate in the private and public debate over the theological foundations for leadership *before* and *beyond* individual charges and acts. Those who listen only to the anguished voice of the victim cannot be expected to appreciate the fine points of theological arguments for the tenacity of God's call to leadership or the indelible stamp of ordination. But church leaders must be prepared to defend the integrity of the church's language and practice in the face of the skepticism of a secular public. There are truths about church leadership that do not lend themselves to seven-second sound bites on the evening news.

Recent revelations of sexual abuse and cover-up in the church reveal the dysfunction of a closed and self-protecting organization: a church succumbed to its own pride. Such a breakdown may require government intervention on behalf of the victim. But such intervention should be the extraordinary exception, not the rule. It does not, or should not, negate the good intentions and capacity of the church to act as a responsible moral community as much as possible without outside intervention. From the New Testament's instructions to Christians to take their grievances to the saints rather than the courts (1 Cor. 6:1-8) and to restore the punished believer to fellowship (2 Cor. 2:5-8), to the latest edition of any given denomination's polity,[15] there is a stated vision of the church as a community that practices justice. The church can and should deal with its moral conflict internally as far as possible and as long as possible. Going outside the church, for example, appealing to the state for resolution in noncriminal cases, is viewed as a breakdown in that community. The contemporary church through its polities and practices must continue to imagine the possibility of an alternative community that can care for its moral problems internally, including the problem of a fallen leader.

David will never be the same after the Bathsheba episode; there are too many severe losses. But David remains the leader chosen by God and some of the most strategic moments of his leadership of God's people lie ahead.

CHAPTER NINE

PRIVATE TEARS, PUBLIC FACES

2 Samuel 18:31–19:8

Then the king got up and took his seat in the gate. The troops were all told, "See, the king is sitting in the gate"; and all the troops came before the king. (19:8)

With the confidence of engineers of the human enterprise today's church leaders look for that "healthy balance" of family and career, home and work, private and public selves. The prophetic church-leader-slash-soccer-mom never misses a game. Her daughter grows up to be an astronaut. The happily married pastor knows his twelve hundred parishioners by name yet carefully monitors his teenage son's mood swings and changing circle of friends. The son grows up to be a well-adjusted language arts teacher.

Wherever clergy gather these days, in breakfast gatherings, at professional meetings, or continuing education events, questions of self-care and balance edge out questions of call and sacrifice. How do you keep your Sabbath? What helps you maintain boundaries? Does your spouse resent all your evening meetings? Are you taking off enough time? Do your children resent you for the things you love as a leader in the church? The peer pressure on these occasions is to confess to work addiction and share ways of keeping it in check. A favorite group pastime is dissecting the what-a-shame stories of successful pastors whose marriages or family ties were apparent casualties of their dedication to the call to church leadership.

There are parallel sentiments heard in the secular workplace today, and echoes of it reach the secular leadership literature. The man (usually) of the GI generation who climbs the corporate ladder, compulsively dedicated to the company and emotionally distant from his family, is becoming extinct. The scenario of lifelong commitment to the same employer, where extraordinary sacrifices of personal time lead to seniority and promotion, are being replaced by scenarios of routine change of employers and even multiple careers. In addition, marriages where both partners work are the norm and they demand a more equitable sharing of the responsibilities for children or aging parents. Time taken for closer parenting or retooling for the next phase of work have become fairly routine interruptions in career trajectories.

Rising leaders in the secular fields hope to find employers or occupations that will accommodate the pull of family connections they carry into the workplace. Peter Senge imagines progressive companies "ending the war between work and family"[1] by emphasizing work/home integration as a desired trait of leadership, by making it acceptable for persons to acknowledge family issues in the midst of business issues, and by providing counseling support on family issues. "One cannot build a learning organization on a foundation of broken homes and strained relationships."[2]

Wherever clergy gather these days to ask their serious questions of self-care and balance there is often someone in the group holding back. She's thinking, "It's not that simple." He wants to shout, "You've got it all backwards." But they don't know how to say what they're feeling without sounding anachronistic. So they allow their silence to become another layer added to the already thick curtain suspended between their private lives and public faces.

A woman in the group wants to argue that the vision that you can "have it all," rewarding work and rewarding family life at the same time, is only a mirage, another desperate projection of the American dream of the promised land. The reality is "a nightmare of anxiety, tension, and strife. Social, economic, and even legal structures punish women who choose procreation and nurture over production alone, and they discourage men from becoming more than marginally involved in the activities that give and sustain life."[3]

Her male counterpart in the group wants to confess last night's shouting match that occurred at the parsonage as he tried to justify the pastoral call that pulled him away from yet another family event. He wishes he could admit that he often experiences ministry and marriage as two totalitarian claims pulling in opposite directions. The conflict depletes his confidence as a church leader and as a husband and father. But to make such an admission, especially before a group of one's peers, could be detrimental to his career. So he remains silent.

No one, not even the crustiest member of the GI generation who denies any regrets over not being more present to his children, could be against the contemporary calls for wholeness in the practice of church leadership. We all hunger for what theologians from Augustine to James Gustafson have called "well-ordered loves."[4]

But what if the new anxieties for balance between career and home life, the ideal of "having it all together" are premature? And what if the right ordering of our loves is not some amicable self-help project but an intense struggle of mountains and valleys that leaves us pleading for some provision of grace? First and Second Samuel, like the Bible elsewhere (e.g., 1 Cor. 7:25-40), is more realistic than today's society about the clash of covenants for those called to lead the people of God. As we will see with David and Absalom, there is no sidestepping the tangled webs of the heartstrings of human love. As we will also see with David and God, the call to go out before the people does not go away even when it proves inconvenient or difficult.

Listening to the Books of Samuel

Part of the universal appeal of 1 and 2 Samuel is the degree to which their stories allow us to see the human side of characters involved in the great dramas of leadership at a crucial time for Israel. Private relationships and public roles often come into tension and must be balanced. The successful public leader is not always so successful at making wise personal decisions. Personal trials sometimes intrude on public responsibility because of those decisions.

Eli, the kindly and pious priest, is unable to control his corrupt sons. He well knows they jeopardize the future of his house. Yet, in the midst of personal anguish he still must act faithfully and raise Samuel to be the prophet Israel needs in a time of crisis (1 Sam. 2–3). Samuel's own sons are not worthy successors of his leadership. So Samuel must obey God's command to anoint kings in spite of his view that the request of the people for a king is sinful (1 Sam. 8). In his day, Jonathan swears a covenant of friendship to David, and he and his sister Michal help David escape the crazed jealousy of Saul. Yet, Jonathan's role as prince and his duty to his father and his people demand that he remain with Saul to march into a battle doomed from its start (1 Sam. 19–20; 31).

David's story, almost from its beginning, is marked by the tensions between his growing responsibilities as leader of God's people and the personal life we are allowed to see in all its pathos. He must abandon the love of Jonathan and Michal in order to preserve his life and pursue his destiny as God's anointed (1 Sam. 19–20). His grief over the death of Jonathan and Saul must give way to the demands of a kingdom that now becomes his responsibility (2 Sam. 1). Later, even in the midst of royal responsibilities, he honors his covenant of friendship with Jonathan by caring for Jonathan's son Mephibosheth (2 Sam. 9). Later still, faced with the weight of God's judgment for adultery and murder (2 Sam. 11–12), David grieves over the dying son born to Bathsheba but must resume his public duties when the child dies: "I shall go to him but he will not return to me" (2 Sam. 12:23).

David's life continues with a series of personal tragedies: the rape of his daughter Tamar, the murder of Amnon by Absalom in revenge for the rape of his half sister, the banishment of Absalom for this murder, Absalom's return but the lack of reconciliation, and finally Absalom's outright rebellion as he attempts to seize the throne from David (2 Sam. 13–18). Through all of this David must still be king and leader of his people. He is a loving but flawed father, husband, friend, and believer; but through all his personal struggles he still has public responsibility. With Absalom's death this fragile tension between the private and public almost breaks.

In spite of Absalom's treachery, David had pleaded with his commanders to spare Absalom's life. But when Joab comes upon Absalom hanging helplessly, his hair caught in a tree, Joab kills him (2 Sam. 18:9-15). The narrative continues with the aftermath of Absalom's death. The tragic news of the son's death is brought to the waiting father, and David's consuming grief threatens to overwhelm the effect of the victory. The pathos of this grief is portrayed in a graphic man- ner that has touched the hearts of generations that have read this story and made it a virtual icon of parental anguish. "O my son Absalom, my son, my son Absalom! Would I had died instead of you, O Absalom, my son, my son" (18:33).

David's role as father, protecting even a rebellious son, is allowed to prevail over any portrait of him as a ruthless king putting down a rebellion against his rule. The story builds dramatically to the moment David receives the tragic news of Absalom's death. Thirteen verses (18:19-32) stretch the tension as rival runners bring word to an anxious father who pleads for news of the welfare of the son. David almost dismisses word of the victory seeking news of Absalom. When David learns of Absalom's death the magnitude of his grief entirely obscures any response to the victory (18:33). It remains for Joab to see the demoralizing effect of David's grief on his supporters who feel belittled by the reception of their service in behalf of him and his throne. Joab, in his usual direct way, confronts David and coaxes him to resume the role of king in spite of his pain (19:1-8). The need for leadership remains in spite of the great per- sonal anguish. The exercise of that leadership cannot be suspended indefinitely.

The heart-rending scene of David's grief over Absalom's death is a scene of such universal human pathos that it has attracted unusual attention from ancient times to our own era. The tragic moment addresses the reader on multiple levels.

1. First and foremost David feels the depths of a father's grief at the loss of a son. Whatever the circumstances, whatever the strains on the relationship, every parent can sympathize with the pain of having one's own child die first. Many know and recognize the cry of David's loss without understanding any of the complexities of the relationship between David and Absalom. David's poignant state- ment that he would willingly have died in Absalom's place has become particularly emblematic of parental willingness to sacrifice one's own welfare to preserve the life of one's child. The story of

Absalom's rebellion may seem particularly relevant to parents of children who take self-destructive paths from which parental love, though willing to sacrifice, cannot save them. The power of this portrait of parental grief gives this moment in David's story a familiarity and emotional identification that function apart from the complexities of the story in 2 Samuel. Part of the message of this story is conveyed in the realization that leaders are also vulnerable human beings. Crises, struggles, loss, and pain invade the lives of leaders as surely as the lives of any other person, and the power of these moments must be honored and respected. It is well for leaders to recognize their own vulnerability as a constant element to be given its due rather than to be blindsided in the midst of a crisis.

2. The text, however, points beyond emotional identification with parental loss (or any other human crisis) to some of the deeper issues encompassed in this climactic moment of David's grief. David is caught in a tension between his roles as father and as king. Absalom is a rebel and a traitor against the king; nevertheless, the father loves him. Earlier, David, alienated from Absalom, had called him only "the young man Absalom" (18:5), but now Absalom is "my son," and David utters this phrase repeatedly (five times) in anguish and grief.

David is caught in a tragic conflict between public and private roles. As king he must regard Absalom as a criminal whose fate is deserved, but as father he cannot accept such an end for his son. As king he has vast power to influence events, but as a grief-stricken father he has no power to bring his son back to life. Frederick Buechner reminds us that when David wished he had died instead of Absalom, "he meant it, of course. If he could have done the boy's dying for him, he would have done it. If he could have paid the price for the boy's betrayal of him, he would have paid it. If he could have given his own life to make the boy alive again, he would have given it. But even a king can't do things like that. As later history was to prove, it takes a God."[5]

This poignant moment in David's story is a reminder to us of the difficulty of balancing public responsibility and familial loyalty. Like David we often learn to love when it is too late. When David's love would have made a difference he was only the king—allowing Absalom's return but not allowing access to the father's love (2 Sam. 14). In our own society the lesson of David's grief is not simply a matter of personal relationships but of public leadership able to respond to private needs in relationship. David's human emotions became visible when it was too late. In his story one wonders what might have been avoided if David's heart had overflowed with love and forgiveness at an earlier moment rather than with grief after Absalom is gone. Leaders cannot ignore the balancing of public and private responsibilities that is necessary to deal with the crises that will come in either or both arenas. David needed to be both king and father in a consistent way. Instead he was the king when Absalom needed a father; and he was a father when it was too late, and yet he must still be the king.

3. But David's weeping may, in part, be for himself as well as Absalom. David's suffering and loss are not innocent. It is David's own model of grasping, arrogant power that Absalom has emulated. It is judgment on David's sin that is playing itself out in the tragedies of his family. This drama of sin and judgment, passing tragically from fathers to sons, is a theme that has attracted the attention of Christian writers from Augustine to the present. They found in this final scene of the drama of Absalom's rebellion a tragic and sobering outcome to the conflict between the exercise of self-interested human free will and the irresistible workings of divine providence. This they believed was a perennial tension in human existence lived within the framework of divine will. Absalom's loss was not just a human tragedy but a result of divine justice. It may well be that this scene continues to have a tragic pertinence for modern leaders for this same reason. David's grief speaks to us not simply of parental loss but of his recognition that his own sins, Absalom's sins, and God's justice have all helped bring this tragic moment to pass. We recognize in David's grief our own grief over many losses that we have not experienced simply as victims but as perpetrators. How much greater the grief when we know that we have helped bring its cause. It is the despair of our soul coupled to the grief of our heart.

Absalom went to war against his father in an effort to seize for himself the place he had lost by imitating the violence that his own father had used to get what he desired. This vicious cycle is not unknown to the parents and children of every generation. We know that we have modeled behavior and values that subsequent generations will imitate—to our sorrow. If we identify with the grief of David over his son it is because we too often experience it as our own, or that of others close to us.

This scene of David's desolation will forever touch the human heart with its portrait of a father's pain. One can hope that it will also remind us that time can run out. There are stories where the prodigal son does not come home and the waiting father's embrace is empty.

Although David's story focuses on a father and a son, it stands as a reminder to those who exercise leadership: private lives and public responsibilities can never be totally separated. The leader stands before his public filled with a private history. The leader draws from her history, God-given gifts, and the grace that comes from the positive ways she has been shaped by healthy relationships, but she is also burdened by the crises and failures that are a part of every personal story to some degree. Leaders cannot ignore this tension of public and private. Failure to tend to both roles responsibly leads only to tragedy. In David's moment of crisis he is unable to be father or king.

4. The final part of this episode has received less attention but is very important when we reflect on the public and private roles that leaders must play simultaneously. In his private grief David loses sight of his people and their reliance on his leadership. It is Joab who must remind him that the very people whose service has saved his life and kingdom are being treated by David as if their service has not mattered, as if they have wounded David rather than saved him (2 Sam. 19:1-8). When personal crises come into the lives of leaders, as they surely must, it is important to realize that a leader's public role is still carried with the leader. David the grieving father nevertheless still is the king. He cannot cease being the king. Pastors in times of crisis do not cease being the pastor. To be sure, a leader cannot ignore the weight of personal loss or stress and cannot be expected to give the same focus to public responsibilities as in normal times. Yet, careless inattention to ongoing public responsibility can wound other lives, undo good work done over years, and damage the future effectiveness of leadership. We do not take our public roles on and off as if they were clothing. The wounded pastor is still the pastor even while hurting from the wounds.

The good news is that we may discover, as did David, that the very people we lead can give crucial personal support in such difficult times if we have not allowed ourselves to become isolated in moments of private pain. The very act of being king/pastor/ leader includes a human connectedness beyond institutional responsibility. Our vulnerability is not a private matter alone but is to some degree a sharing of public vulnerability as well. By such sharing, leadership can grow stronger. The effort to be leaders while our pain is visible forges new bonds of community. To become submerged in pain or isolated in pain as if the community does not exist is perceived by the leader's people as a failure of trust and creates distance and separation. As wounded leaders willing to lead in and through our own woundedness, we create new possibilities for the community. Such leadership models the hope the church holds out to every person: in the very midst of our brokenness God offers us new life.

The Church Leader's Children

The realism about the family life of leaders in the books of Samuel must be given its due. It deserves its place in the canon of scripture alongside the more optimistic prescriptions of Proverbs or the household codes of the Pastoral Letters. Leaders may have children who may become obstinate, prodigal, or even rebellious. Leaders may suffer the loss of a child and become immobilized in grief. Tragedy happens! And still, leaders must go on and go out.

Walter was driven. Called, yes, but also driven. While at seminary his intelligence and ability to obsess on a project were recognized by his Old Testament professor who encouraged him to pursue a Ph.D. But Walter maintained a steady course for the pastorate partly out of conviction that he belonged there and partly out of the urgent need to provide for a growing family that eventually included four boys. Walter's energy registered in marathons of daily visitations in hospitals and homes. His intelligence sparkled in sermons rich with literary metaphors and quotations at a time when the congregation still connected with such allusions. Though Walter tended to keep close to his own church and avoid denominational gatherings his quality work caught the eye of others. He was assigned to larger parishes with greater demands, eventually becoming senior pastor at one of the conference's largest churches.

Ruth was Walter's lifelong companion. She was second generation British, refined and determined to find an identity apart from the minister's wife. Before marriage she earned a degree to teach social science and as the four boys became independent she began to do more and more substitute teaching. One of the sacrifices she paid to Walter's itinerant ministry was her inability to secure a tenured position, but the boys, the church, and the day or two a week teaching provided enough challenges to her considerable energy.

All four of Walter and Ruth's sons graduated from the same United Methodist college as their father. The first went on to become a medical doctor, specializing in psychiatric disorders. The next son became a high school social science teacher. The third son answered a call to ministry and was attending seminary when a brain tumor was discovered; it took his life in a matter of months. The youngest son seemed to have the hardest time finding direction and suffered from long seasons of depression. On a whim he went to Atlanta to join a protest led by Martin Luther King, Jr. Somehow he drifted away from the event and eventually found himself parked overlooking the lights of Atlanta in the dark. Alone as ever, he stuffed rags in the car's exhaust, rolled up the windows, and surrendered to death.

Walter and Ruth never recovered from the deaths of their two youngest sons only months apart. Walter especially suffered from doubts and self-recriminations regarding the son who had committed suicide. Was Walter's love of work somehow related to the loss of a son? Was he too busy to pick up some final signal of distress?

Walter and Ruth had the personal counsel of their friend, a nationally recognized authority in grief at that time. They worked hard to claim the *process* of grief recently introduced to the public in the work of Elisabeth Kübler-Ross. But nothing worked, and the pain went on and on. In the late fall of the year Walter slipped on a curb and suffered multiple hip and leg fractures. He was confined to the house for weeks while winter set in. As the snow fell and wind blew outside the parsonage, inside Walter and Ruth rehearsed their losses over and over, like detectives rechecking evidence for the clue that sheds light. In the course of those brooding interrogations Walter began to talk about taking retirement.

Walter and Ruth began to daydream about a retirement home near the Amish farms. Their conversation opened the floodgates of memory to years of stored-up resentments: Friday nights tied up in wedding rehearsals rather than high school football games with the boys, make-do parsonages with never enough bedrooms, and the endless interruptions of evening meals by phone calls that could have waited.

The high tide of regret had just about finished its work when a strong riptide kicked in. In the course of jointly composing Walter's letter requesting retirement a reservoir of countervailing memories began to surface. There were persons who answered the call to ministry while Walter was their pastor. Couples he counseled through crisis that remained married. There were youth awakened to their gifts, allies formed in the fierce battles over sanctuary renovation, and saints walked alongside as they crossed over to death. There were sermons that connected, some even published, and there were unforgettable worship experiences at Christmas and Easter. Walter and Ruth had to admit to the sensation of being swept up and swept along by a larger drama that gave meaning to their lives.

Our personal stories and private lives must be located within a canopy of larger movements. All our experiences and all our actions ache for the larger web of interpretation. Life was never only about Walter and Ruth and their boys. It never is in ministry. The combination of marriage and ministry at its best tends to be what William Willimon describes as constructively symbiotic. It feeds off experiences outside of the marriage, strengthened precisely because of its rich network of other important commitments.[6] The high and low experiences of leading the people of God become irreplaceable content in the complex, colorful, sometimes conflicted, and often humorous narrative that a healthy parsonage marriage is. This unique connection of personal well-being with wider social goods was introduced forever into the theology of church leadership by the Reformers.[7] And it must be defended perpetually against the doctrine of a celibate clergy on the one hand and a disregard for marriage's "important social, intergenerational, and public dimensions" on the other.[8]

Walter did retire that June. But instead of moving into their retirement home Walter and Ruth moved into another old and eccentric parsonage, and Walter settled in to help a little country church that awoke one day to find itself in the middle of a housing development. The church could not afford a full-time skilled pastor and it was at a critical point of transition. Walter was a godsend. And the more he gave the more Walter felt his energy return. Sometimes Ruth would quip about being "a tad younger" than Sarah and Abraham when they started out.

In three years the church was ready to stand on its own. Walter and Ruth moved into their retirement dream home near the Amish farms. The second summer there, Walter suffered a massive stroke while on a walk and died. Two years after that Ruth began to show signs of Alzheimer's. Ten years later she sits in a nursing home and stares blankly. The worth of Ruth and Walter's sacrifices and their mark on the mainline church during the second half of the twentieth century are in the hands of others to tell and in the mind of God who will never forget.

Getting Up and Going Out Again

The troops outside have fought so valiantly and now look expectantly for some sign of their leader's recognition. The leader inside is overcome with paralyzing personal grief. "O my son Absalom, O Absalom, my son, my son!" Enter Joab. The volatile and outspoken commander confronts David with his public destiny and public obligation: "So go out at once and speak kindly to your servants" (2 Sam. 19:7). David shakes himself out of the hold of his personal suffering, puts on the symbols of his office, then goes out to the gate to salute the troops.

Ellis, as they say, "comes from good stock." His father was a second-career pastor who left a profitable hardware business in answer to the call. He took some crash courses in Bible, theology, and preaching; then he went out and faithfully served small churches scattered along the ridges and valleys of north central Pennsylvania. When Ellis's own call to ministry came, his father determined the son would have better preparation for service. Ellis attended college and then a strong Methodist seminary on the East Coast. As a pastor he soon gained a reputation for his thoughtful preaching, pastoral heart, and work ethic. His indefatigable attention to detail, whether over a parishioner's medical condition or a blueprint for a new sanctuary, became legend. Ellis served some of the largest churches in his annual conference and served a term as a superintendent of pastors. At one time or another he chaired three of the more important administrative committees of the annual conference.

About two-thirds of the way through that career Ellis's wife Dorothy was diagnosed with and began to experience the repercussions of multiple sclerosis. In time Dorothy would be confined to a wheelchair and the symptoms of that chronic degenerative disease of the central nervous system would become more pronounced. The intrusion of MS was the defining crisis for Dorothy and Ellis. It demanded an escalating series of accommodations. It became a more pronounced competitor to the demands of active ministry.

For the last decade of his full-time service Ellis worked every angle of a pastor's flextime for Dorothy's sake: maximizing use of an office in the house, squeezing her doctor's appointments into the lunch hour, recasting distant commitments into day trips that required commuting heroics.

After retirement Ellis was asked to serve as the bishop's administrative assistant on a part-time basis. Most of his colleagues thought Ellis would not accept that invitation. It was an obvious affirmation of his gifts, but it did not seem congruous with the growing need to be more available to Dorothy as her physical powers dissipated. Surely Ellis would be relieved to give up the juggling act.

At Dorothy's insistence Ellis accepted the position of the bishop's administrative assistant. Those who did not know the couple might analyze his motives or their marriage. Those who did know them knew better, including their grown children who followed in their footsteps of public service, one a pastor and the other a teacher. Ellis and Dorothy cherish their privacy but find meaning in the call to ministry that interrupts. It is a shared meaning of personal fulfillment in public service, a loss of self for the sake of participation in something greater. It is not easy to explain in a culture of individual fulfillment and "bowling alone"[9] because it exists in conspicuous obliqueness to that culture.

These days Dorothy putters at the lowered counters Ellis designed for their retirement home. On really good days she can pick up her brushes and return to her oil and canvas. She paints landscapes that have become increasingly difficult for her to get out and view. She paints roses with an attention to minuscule detail of someone looking for the elusive secret of their visual beauty. She talks on the phone to a large connection of colleagues in ministry and favorite parishioners accrued through the years. She receives regular progress reports and visits from her grown children and the growing grandchildren. She is occupied, and most days the long hours Ellis still devotes to the work of ministry pass quickly.

And Ellis juggles on, daily tending to the needs of his companion of a lifetime and receiving her support and encouragement as he daily answers the call to ministry from which there really is no retirement.

On Not Having It All Together

It is time to exchange the exaggerated claims for wholeness in ministry, claims that often censor the voice of private frustrations and more often dismiss the importance of public commitments, for the more helpful realism of the books of Samuel. There are leaders of the people of God who faithfully lead yet do not "have it all together." In their private lives they may experience tension or bear crosses, but they obey a voice that calls them also to invest in the struggles for a common good. So they wash away the private tears and they go out before the people. And as it is with the imperfect creatures all around us in nature—birds missing tail feathers, spiders missing legs, squirrels with damaged tails—once you slow down enough to notice one you begin to notice dozens.

A clergy couple takes turns caring for their severely handicapped adult son. They worry who will care for him in the future if something happens to them as each in turn rushes out the door for the next hospital call or trustees meeting.

The wife of a pastor suffers from severe chronic depression requiring occasional hospitalization. There are good days when she is a lively partner for conversation about her husband's work. She takes interest in their teenage children and helps with the cooking and cleaning. But many days she is quiet and withdrawn, and too often the pastor must go out to meet the needs of others from a home life that has depleted rather than replenished his emotional resources for the work of ministry. Over and over again, he does this.

A judicatory leader leaves at home an invalid husband every time she goes out the door. On a given night she may travel to a distant church in the mountainous region of the area she serves to conduct a difficult meeting. The people in that church have little respect for either the denomination or her office. She battles through the meeting and drives home. Her husband, dying from AIDS received through a blood transfusion, waits up to greet her. He will serve her Earl Grey tea as they replay her evening. She will quote some of the more colorful remarks from the meeting, mimicking the gruff voices of the people in attendance challenging her composure. She will hold up her emotional self-awareness and leadership practices for scrutiny. He will recount the televised evening news. She will tell of almost hitting a deer on the winding mountain road on the way home. They will laugh together feeling like two city slickers far from home. In the morning she will get up and once again go out to follow her unyielding vocation.

They are everywhere, these persons whose private lives make their public commitments even more difficult and stressful. They wear gracious faces that hide as well as reveal. They are pastors serving the little rural church off the main road and they are bishops in cosmopolitan centers. The main thing is they are present and accounted for when the moment for action arrives. Easy prescriptions for wholeness in ministry do not begin to address the reality of these complex lives filled with difficult choices. Those prescriptions project a David who is a skilled engineer of human relationships at home and abroad. Second Samuel offers instead a portrait of a parent broken by grief and remorse, washing his tear-stained face and going out to encourage his troops.

CHAPTER TEN

LEADING FROM PROVIDENCE

2 Samuel 22:1-51
He brought me out into a broad place; he delivered me,
because he delighted in me. . . . Indeed, you are my lamp,
O LORD, the LORD lightens my darkness. By you I can
crush a troop, and by my God I can leap over a wall.
(22:20, 29-30)

At no point is the distance between most contemporary accounts of leadership (secular or religious) and the account of leadership given in 1 and 2 Samuel greater than when it comes to the subject of providence. By most contemporary accounts the leader should ask the sort of questions that clear up the fog and reveal a clear path forward to a specific destination. What traits do I need to be successful? Where are the models of excellence? What information must I process? What corporate culture must I penetrate? Where are the landmines? How accurate is our feedback system? What nostalgia is holding us back? What vision will propel us forward? What may we extrapolate from the present to prepare for our future?

According to the books of Samuel leadership is not about clearing up a fog or, to use a preferable word, a mystery. Leadership is about learning to accept that mystery and to live well within it. In the fecund language of William Cowper's 1774 hymn on providence, leadership means being absorbed by the questions arising from one overriding fact: "God Moves in a Mysterious Way."[1] Are the ominous clouds on the horizon actually "big with mercy," and will those clouds "break in blessings" on our heads? Can I stop projecting the fears of "feeble sense" on the Lord long enough to glimpse the "smiling face" that lies "behind a frowning providence"? Am I strong enough to break rank from those who "scan his work in vain" because of their unbelief? Will I allow God the courtesy of interpreting what God is up to because I hope that one day God "will make it plain"?

Leaders are normally consumed by action. By one well-known contemporary account the daily activities of a chief executive are characterized by "brevity, variety, and discontinuity." Barely half of their activities engage them for as long as nine minutes. They may average 583 activities in an eight hour day, mostly collecting, processing, and transmitting soft information; negotiating potential or actual conflict; and attending the rituals and ceremonies of the organization. Only 10 percent of these activities will last as long as an hour.[2]

Yet every leader carries some ultimate interpretation of who they are and what they do. It is a portable inner vision of self in the world. It is the stash of the pieces of their lives and the weaving together of those pieces into a narrative that gives perspective to the relentless daily practice. For some church leaders the interpretation of self in the world is still beneath the surface of speech. All they know for sure is how much they are *not like* the persons being described in some of the most popular literature of leadership and management. They hunger for an interpretation that has more to do with mystery and drama than those glib profiles of success.[3]

For most leaders the interpretation of self in the world is a positive exercise of the imagination, even if only carried out at the edge of consciousness. It has the character of what one prominent writer on leadership calls "the Dream," a vague sense of self in the world that generates energy and a sense of life as adventure.[4] The Dream is "more formal than a pure fantasy, yet less articulated than a fully thought-out plan." For the church leader this might mean viewing herself or himself in such a character as a rescuer, defender, mover and shaker, midwife, wizard, gardener, or coach.

For church leaders the Dream must be placed within a narrative of providence, the fabric of God's larger purposes and movements. The Dream is more than a self-referenced project of determination and action. The Dream is a gift of experience and reflection that arises out of the drama of leading the people of God. It is God who gives to church leadership its integrity, and God's actions in real time that give to church leadership its weight. To be a church leader is to theologize; to lead well is to theologize incessantly. The books of Samuel have modeled the practice throughout. What power behind the stars responds to social chaos by sending a leader? Who ultimately calls leaders and coaxes them toward their futures? Who finally judges leaders when they err and holds them to account when they repent? From whom do leaders receive their visions for a just society and their inspirations for compassion? How shall leaders manage their hungers and order their loves? And now here at their end, the books of Samuel raise the God question once again, this time as the ultimate factor in the practice of church leadership.

Listening to the Books of Samuel

The psalm of thanksgiving in 2 Samuel 22 is attributed to David at a time near the end of his life "when the LORD delivered him from the hand of all his enemies, and from the hand of Saul" (v. 1). It is a duplicate of Psalm 18. It stands as a complement to the Song of Hannah (1 Sam. 2:1-10), and the two songs together bracket the stories of leadership in the books of Samuel with the celebration of God's providence. That providence is the ultimate reality behind the human successes and failures in the leadership of Saul and David. Hannah's song anticipates that God, who can reverse the powers of the world, nevertheless has chosen to work through a king, God's anointed one (1 Sam. 2:10). Second Samuel 22 is set as David's own song looking back over a career of success and failure, gift and grasp, blessing and curse—and finding there the steady hand of God's sovereignty and grace in it all.

David's psalm in 2 Samuel 22 falls into three parts that together testify to the main theme of the books of Samuel and provide the final key to understanding leadership of God's people. The first section (vv. 1-2) is a thanksgiving in celebration of God's power to deliver from chaos. It focuses on the grace-filled activity of God's salvation. The second section (vv. 21-28) extols human moral virtue and the power of righteousness to gain the Lord's favor. In verse 24, David proclaims "I was blameless before him." The emphasis is on human ability to claim God's grace by virtue of one's own righteousness.

Section three of this psalm, verses 29-51, serves as a corrective to the impression given by the first two sections alone. In the king's voice, God's ultimate power is acknowledged as central; in verse 29: "Indeed you are my lamp, O LORD; the LORD lightens my darkness." But immediately following is an affirmation of David's own abilities and deeds in verse 30: "By you I can crush a troop, and by my God I can leap over a wall." The verses that follow are filled with first-person affirmations of heroic deeds and mighty acts of leadership against enemies and over obstacles: "I crush . . . leap over . . . pursued . . . destroyed . . . did not turn back . . . consumed . . . struck down . . . they fell" (vv. 30, 38-39). Yet, constantly alongside the deeds of the royal "I," the psalm acknowledges the divine, empowering "Thou." The leader achieves great things through admirable abilities, but all that he does is enabled by the grace-filled activity of God, who deserves to be praised ("by you . . . by my God" v. 30). God's salvation is crucial (vv. 1-20) and human gifts are required (vv. 21-28), but the entirety of the books of Samuel emphasizes leadership as the unique combination of divine providence with human personality through which God has chosen to work. This is the emphasis that is at the center of the climactic third section of this psalm (vv. 29-51).

This psalm still speaks to us of the context in which we must exercise leadership for the church. We have retained a sense of the invading reality of chaos and its threat to our attempts to find ordered meaning for our lives. During the years of work on this manuscript terrorists damaged the Pentagon in Washington, D.C., and destroyed the twin towers in New York. Anthrax arrived in our post offices, snipers shot down innocent people in our neighborhoods, and our children and friends went off to war twice—in Afghanistan and Iraq. We know the reality of chaos, but we have lost touch with the corresponding language of deliverance, the elemental way this psalm speaks its conviction that God's power can drive back the chaos. We live in a time when we are enamored of our own human capacities. When these capacities fail to deliver us from crises in our daily lives, our world, and our institutions, we often discover that we have lost touch with a sense of divine power. Only that power is capable of driving back the darkness, restoring order in the midst of chaos, and surprising us with the grace of life when we feel overpowered by death.

In terms of this psalm, our generation in the church (reflecting our culture) prefers the ordered, moral universe suggested by the second section of this psalm (vv. 21-28). The cool, rational, didactic approach of obeying commandments and seeking righteousness tempts us into thinking that by our own efforts we can control chaos. For example, in the face of difficult and divisive moral issues (sexual orientation, abortion, racism) or challenges such as the shape of the family, economic inequities, and the proliferation of violence, the church's leadership is prone to establish study commissions. It passes carefully worded resolutions, seeks new legislation that defines righteousness, and devises pragmatic programs of action. One of the teachings of this psalm may be that such leadership approaches to the vexing challenges of our day only have their place in the context of a more elemental confidence and celebration of God's singular power to overcome chaos and to establish the Kingdom. Such a confidence in the decisive role of God's providence may let us regard our own leadership efforts as less ultimate and self-sufficient. Such a confidence will require a boldness of speech about God's salvation that recognizes that our own leadership efforts remain important, but cannot save us apart from God's providence working through us and in spite of us if necessary.

This psalm located at the end of the books of Samuel is a final comment on leadership as a unique combination of divine providence and human agency. It is not an idealized story of unblemished heroes and glossed-over failures. In the end, David is a model for our leadership in both positive and negative ways. His career as leader, God's anointed one, divides into two parts at the point of his adultery with Bathsheba and the murder of Uriah. It has been said that David's story is first one of blessing and then one of curse. His life is blessed at first by his sense of receiving God's gift. He recognizes God's grace in the events that bring him to leadership. What at first separates David as a leader from Saul and others is his constant awareness that whatever his gifts and capacities, his successes and failures, it is God who makes the difference. He prays constantly; he counts on God to make the difference, whether for deliverance, or comfort, or guidance—and when he has fallen in sin, even for forgiveness (Ps. 51). David praises; he petitions; he confesses; he intercedes; he trusts. Whatever his own gifts, David knows he is surrounded by the gift of God's providence working to establish the kingdom. He is not alone and his leadership is not dependent only on his resources.

But, as we have seen, David's sense of gift gives way to grasp. He uses his power for his own self-centered purposes and closes himself off from his sense of God's presence and providence. God's judgment through the prophet Nathan and the tragedy of his sons' violent self-centeredness (imitating their father) bring David to the point of brokenness and failure as a leader. Only then does David reclaim his confidence in God's providence as a resource for leadership. In his retreat from Jerusalem to escape the rebellious hand of his own son Absalom, David seems to recognize what he has lost as a center for his leadership of God's people. In 2 Samuel 15:25, he tells his followers, "If I find favor in the eyes of the LORD, he will bring me back and let me see both [the ark] and the place where it stays. But if he says, 'I take no pleasure in you,' here I am, let him do to me what seems good to him." A few verses later, in verse 31, David is praying again, reconnected with the true source of his leadership.

It is not accidental that David's name is connected with the psalms. This is not so much a claim of authorship as it is a sense that David's leadership throughout the events of his life is enfolded in worship. It is an expansive view of worship. It encompasses praise and thanksgiving, lament and petition. It is in the connection of David's name to the psalms that even his time of sin with Bathsheba is enfolded in the providential grace of God's forgiveness (Ps. 51). Psalm 18, the duplicate of David's concluding psalm in 2 Samuel 22, is surrounded in the psalter by psalms carrying the name of David that elaborate the images of leadership carried out in awareness and partnership with God's providential action in the midst of God's people for the sake of God's mission in the world.

In the end, the psalm of 2 Samuel 22 recommends the rediscovery of a leadership in the church that enfolds itself in worship, prayer, and a consciousness of the difference made by God's providence. This psalm declares that God chooses to make Israel's salvation—and ours—a divine-human enterprise. The "I" of genuine church leadership that lives up to its calling must confess that what enables wholeness and success in human efforts is the power of the divine "Thou." In the Christian faith the word for this confessional reality is *incarnation*. God's "steadfast love" is best known through God's "anointed" (v. 51), through "messiah," the Hebrew term for "anointed one." Christians claim the tradition that Jesus Christ was born in the line of David, that the full meaning of Christ forever includes the story of God acting in, through, and in spite of David.

The model of leadership we see in David foreshadows what we see more fully in the incarnation of God in Jesus Christ. In claiming the incarnation Christians claim the tradition summarized by 2 Samuel 22//Psalm 18 with its concluding celebration of a divine-human partnership through which salvation comes. Hannah's song (1 Sam. 2:1-10) begins the story of God's salvation through David. Mary's song (Luke 1:46-55) echoes it to begin the story of God's salvation through Jesus. We have journeyed through the story of David's leadership and its many dimensions, ending in this final reminder of the crucial difference that rests in God's providence. This psalm of deliverance, obedience, and partnership between God and God's anointed leader David finds its complement in the New Testament claim that Jesus is the one in whom the divine and human are in complete partnership. He is "the son of David."

A Providence for Agents, Not Puppets

God is certainly in ultimate control in the books of Samuel. God has definite preferences about future outcomes. God is determined to have those preferences realized. In the terms of classical and modern theologies of providence, God leans more toward Calvinist images of control than toward Process images of openness. God wills. God knows. God executes plans through both primary and secondary causes; "not a sparrow falls" without God's awareness. It is hard to imagine this God as having only "abstract essence" awaiting "concrete actuality" by humans (the "dipolar theism" of process theology). It is even harder to imagine this God restricted to persuasive rather than coercive action. There is as much of the Unmoved Mover (traditional theology) as of the Most Moved Mover (contemporary theology) in this God. At the end of 2 Samuel and speaking from a lifetime of hard experience David defers to the priority of God's purposes. "If I find favor in the eyes of the LORD, he will bring me back" he says to those who urge him to be more assertive about claiming his rule in Jerusalem (2 Sam. 15:25). It is no longer about David; it is about God. In the words of a contemporary Reformed theologian, David accepts God as "the power that bears down upon us, sustains us, sets an ordering of relationships, provides the conditions of possibilities for human activity and even a sense of direction."[5]

That being said, the picture of providence that emerges in the books of Samuel is not that of Omnipotent and Omniscient Sovereign micromanaging actors and events to comply with a finished script. Again resorting to the classical and modern theologies of providence, the God of Hannah and Eli, Samuel and Michal, David and Bathsheba appears to have *middle knowledge* of events. God not only knows the events that do occur, but also the events that would occur if circumstances were different. God is aware of both facts and *counterfactuals*.[6] If only Eli's children had turned out differently, there would be no need of Samuel. If Saul (Plan A) were up to his calling to leadership, there would be no need of Plan B (David). If David had been out with his army as he should have been in the spring of the year, there would have been no time for the illicit sexual conquest (Bathsheba) and the bleak trail of repercussions that include the death of Uriah. There is a place to where God is headed, but God who respects human freedom and recognizes human frailty appears to be aware of more than one way to get there.

Because God has "middle knowledge," because God in some sense is aware and holds in awareness not only things that are but also things that could be, church leaders are conspicuously human *agents*. They are not puppets fated to play established parts in an already finished drama, as is suggested in much traditional teaching on providence that borrowed freely from Stoic images of predestination.[7] They are agents. They are summoned by a curtain call they may answer or ignore. They can choose whether they will listen to a director whose passion is to bring them "out into a broad place" (2 Sam. 22:20) rather than preserve them in structures of inferiority. They may choose among the parts of the play available to them at any given moment and choose again how well to play the part they select.

Along the way, here and there, God sends prophets or other agents to help. They acquaint church leaders with future plots they had not yet grasped, as Eli does when he helps Samuel translate the voice he hears calling in the night (1 Sam. 3). They remind leaders of alternative scenarios and the probable consequences that follow, as Abigail does when she tries to coax David out of his lethal anger toward Nabal (1 Sam. 25). They hold up a mirror to leaders' stolen scripts and miscast acting, as Nathan does when he confronts the king with his grasping behavior and infidelity (2 Sam. 11). Sometimes these persons are called prophets, other times mentors, consultants, advisors, or simply significant others who will tell it like it is.[8]

Leaders Bent to the Larger Purposes of God

It is the report of 1 and 2 Samuel that there is a benevolent power behind the scenes of the unfolding drama. "It is the Lord (Yahweh) who shapes the events and personalities of this time." All other factors, social, political, economic, geopolitical, and *leadership* "are bent to the divine purpose."[9] Church leaders should receive this report of providence as a word of encouragement. Behind every belligerent Goliath, beside every raging Saul, beyond every insurrectionist Absalom, there stands the Lord who saves us from our enemies.

Church leaders keep themselves grounded in the perspective of providence through the disciplines of theological vision, liturgy, thanksgiving, and story telling.[10] From the perspective of providence, church leaders routinely engage in the practice of reframing what appear to be insurmountable obstacles. Where demographic studies reveal only a declining population, they see the fields white with a harvest of the unchurched. Where a loan officer at the bank calculates their institution to be a high risk, they see a mere matter of untaught stewardship. "Preacher count" (the practice of counting attendance loosely then fudging the numbers upward) is an occupational eccentricity born in a determined hope. Church leaders are nourished by and contribute to an atmosphere of confidence that all the parts will eventually fall into place (Rom. 8:28-30) and so "it ain't over til it's over."

From the perspective of providence, church leaders are always try-ing to locate their stories and the stories of the organizations they serve under the umbrella of God's larger story in history. They con-tinually ask after the "macrostory" to which their "microstories" belong. Church leaders are never quite at home in the local story, theirs or that of the group they serve. In this sense all church lead-ership is basically itinerant and self-effacing. It is not about the leader; it is about God. It is not about only this local congregation; it is about the "one, holy, catholic and apostolic church." And in the end, it is not even only about the "one, holy, catholic and apostolic church"; it is about the future rule of God in the world.[11]

To those of us who have experienced or studied the church in other generations, the contemporary church often appears to be retreating into a local church culture. Listen to the content of the intercessions during worship. Specifically, listen for the omission of larger church issues let alone larger world issues. We have learned specificity and directness in prayer, but we only apply them to "me and mine." Observe how we often translate the ministry of all Christians. It is not a charge to infiltrate work, family, and school with prophetic voice and gospel alternatives. It is an occasion to blur the distinction between clergy and laypersons around matters of preaching, the sacra-ments, and administration. We throw ourselves into short-term expe-riences of hands-on mission in distant places, but are politely silent before the powers and policies that are capable of massively and systemically addressing the squalor of the world's mission situations.

Among several poignant moments captured in the books of Samuel, one of the sharpest comes early in the saga. It is that moment named in 1 Samuel 3:18 when the boy Samuel, who is not yet old enough to identify the voice calling in the night, has been summoned by God as the replacement for Eli and his sons. Samuel reports the call to Eli. The old priest recognizes that he and his household have been dismissed from the unfolding drama of God's larger purposes in history and, in effect, submits to the grim verdict. Someone else must play the part.

In the middle knowledge of God those who show up get to play the game. Sometimes we are ready to "have done with lesser things" and find our better selves in the sacrifices demanded by that game. Sometimes we are not. It is more important that the game go on than that any particular one of us gets to play in it. The game of providence is very serious business.

"Where We Came In": A Personal Reflection from Lew

In the small north central Pennsylvania town where I grew up in the 1950s the Saturday night social event of the summer was the local drive-in theater. The drive-in would open at dusk and cars would begin to trickle in. Couples would park in the back rows, parents with noisy children up front. The children would play on the swings and sliding boards in the last rays of light. An old army jeep would methodically spew billows of insecticide, row by row like a farmer tending corn. When it was dark enough, the projectionist would send images to the huge white wall: previews of coming attrac-tions, news shorts, cartoons, tedious reminders of the junk food avail-able at the concession stand. The main feature was shown twice with an intermission between showings that seemed to go on forever.

My parents would gather and load five sons, one of them infant, and a larder of assorted homemade snacks into a big boat of a car, the Ford Fairlane. We almost never made it to the drive-in in time to view the opening scenes of the first showing of the main feature. That led to one of the few family games we ever sat still long enough to play. While we watched the second showing of the main feature we would debate the point where we arrived during its first showing. "There!" "No, we never saw *that*." "Here! This is where we came in." It was a game of collective memory, recognition, and anticipation. And through my adult years as a church leader I have often thought what good practice it was for responding to any leadership challenge. Collective memory, recognition, and anticipation can help church leaders survive the adjustments of the first years of ministry as much as they can help them navigate the complex struggles and compet-ing covenants that come later, in the prime of their careers. We must figure out where we came in and give ourselves over to the moment in providence given us.

I am "mainline" and spend most of my time leading in the churches and institutions of the mainline denominations, the denominations that have their origin in Europe. A huge cloud of anxiety has descended upon this segment of Christ's church today, like the menacing smoke of a nearby forest fire smothering a city in its path. We spend increasing amounts of energy and resources to maintain the properties and organizational cultures of an earlier and more vital generation. We recognize and report lower attendance numbers. We cut budgets and lay off personnel. We watch ourselves aging without definite prospects of a next generation to carry on the work. Much of our energy that should be directed outward to meet the adaptive challenges of the present moment is dissipated by internal battles over styles of worship or debates such as normalizing homosexuality. We feel a vague sense of guilt over losing the prophetic public voice we once had. We have become awkward in the presence of our evangelical heritage. We are beginning to openly acknowledge that the cutting edge of our denominations may have shifted to other countries on other continents.

Some church leaders in the "mainline" churches are resigned to present trends. A renewal of our churches would require a "surprising work of God" (Jonathan Edwards's name for revival), and there is just no way of predicting such visits. Others are pretty sure we could reverse present trends with the introduction of certain easy-to-learn techniques.[12] Most of us are somewhere in between, trying the techniques but unconvinced that any number of tools or programs is the final answer. So while we exhaust the techniques we also wait and try to figure out our place in the scheme of God's final purposes for the church, for humanity, and for creation. Where have we come in? What part have we been given to play? In the end it is not about us; it is about God. As John Wesley prays, "[L]et me be employed for you or laid aside for you, exalted for you or brought low for you."[13]

Until our final place in God's larger purposes is disclosed what choice do we have but to give our best to the adaptive challenges before us? If today's church leaders share the "DNA" of the leaders of the books of Samuel, then the repertoire of disciplines for responding to the present moment is fairly self-evident. *Show up. Pay attention. Tell the truth. Duck. Don't grasp.* And most of all don't forget to dance madly as David did. Who knows? In the words of Jonathan to his anxious armor-bearer on the eve of battle with the Philistines: "It may be that the LORD will act for us; for nothing can hinder the LORD from saving by many or by few" (1 Sam. 14:6).

NOTES

Introduction

1. Richard N. Soulen and R. Kendall Soulen, *Handbook of Biblical Criticism*, 3rd edition, revised and expanded (Louisville: Westminster John Knox Press, 2001), 52.

2. Laurie Beth Jones, *Jesus, CEO: Using Ancient Wisdom for Visionary Leadership* (New York: Hyperion Books, 1995), 10-12, 210-12, 271-74.

3. The parameters for an appropriate use of the term "paradigm shift" are specified in Thomas S. Kuhn, *The Structure of Scientific Revolutions*, 3rd edition (Chicago and London: University of Chicago Press, 1962, 1970, 1996), 43-51.

4. For a constructive application of the butterfly effect to liberate leadership for a vision of the organization as an open system see Margaret J. Wheatley, *Leadership and the New Science: Discovering Order in a Chaotic World*, 2nd edition (San Francisco: Berrett-Koehler Publishers, 1999), 120-23. Leaders should learn that "in a nonlinear world, very slight variances, things so small as to be indiscernible, can amplify into completely unexpected results."

1. Drinking Water from Our Own Wells

1. David L. Bartlett, *Ministry in the New Testament* (Minneapolis: Fortress Press, 1993; Eugene, Ore.: Wipf and Stock Publishers reprint, 2001), 27-31, 39-45, 48-53, 64-71, 76-82, 97-102, 109-10, 120-23, 126-34, 145-46, 159-62, 167-77.

2. Avery Dulles, *Models of the Church* (Garden City, N.Y.: Doubleday & Company, 1974), 151-65.

3. Thomas C. Oden, *Pastoral Theology: Essentials of Ministry* (San Francisco: Harper & Row, 1983), 49-63.

4. H. Richard Niebuhr with Daniel Day Williams and James M. Gustafson, *The Purpose of the Church and Its Ministry: Reflections on the Aims of Theological Education* (New York: Harper, 1956), 48-94; Robert K. Greenleaf, *Servant Leadership: A Journey into the Nature of Legitimate Power and Greatness* (New York/Mahwah: Paulist Press, 1977, 1991), 218-48.

5. Donald E. Messer, *Contemporary Images of Christian Ministry* (Nashville: Abingdon Press, 1989), 81-169. How eccentric such "contemporary" versions sound a mere decade after their appearance.

6. *Theological Dictionary of the New Testament,* ed. Gerhard Kittel et al., and trans. and ed. Geoffrey W. Bromiley (Grand Rapids, Mich.: William B. Eerdmans, 1964–1976), vol. 6, 700-2.

7. Ibid., vol. 3, 1035-37.

8. Ibid., vol. 2, 608-20.

9. Andrew D. Clarke, *Serve the Community of the Church: Christians as Leaders and Ministers,* First-Century Christians in the Graeco-Roman World Series (Grand Rapids, Mich.: William B. Eerdmans, 2000), 103-41.

10. Ibid., 145-72.

11. Bengt Holmberg, *Paul and Power: the Structure of Authority in the Primitive Church as Reflected in the Pauline Epistles* (Lund, Sweden: CWK Gleerup, 1978; Philadelphia: Fortress Press, 1980), 70-93.

12. Clarke, *Serve the Community,* 202-7, 223-28.

13. Soulen and Soulen, *Handbook of Biblical Criticism,* 72-73.

14. Gerhard Ebeling, *Introduction to a Theological Theory of Language,* trans. R. A. Wilson (Philadelphia: Fortress Press, 1973), 17.

15. I am adapting the threefold typology of the schools of criticism from Soulen and Soulen, 233-35.

16. Paul Tillich, *Systematic Theology: Three Volumes in One* (New York and Evanston: University of Chicago Press, Harper & Row, 1967), vol. 1, 59-66; vol. 2, 13-16.

17. Douglas John Hall, *Thinking the Faith: Christian Theology in a North American Context* (M inneapolis: Augsburg Press, 1989; Fortress Press, 1991), 357-67.

18. Ibid., 158-69, 207-23.

19. Tillich and many of his generation of theologians drew a sharp

distinction between "controlling knowledge" ("It looks upon its object as something which cannot return its look") and participatory or existential knowledge, the knowledge of revelation. The specter of twentieth-century industrialism and its violence (world wars, holocaust, Hiroshima) haunts their epistemology. Tillich, *Systematic Theology*, vol. 1, 97-100, 102-5.

20. Bernard M. Bass, *Bass & Stogdill's Handbook of Leadership: Theory, Research, and Managerial Applications*, 3rd edition (New York: Free Press, 1990), 59-88, 563-703 (trait versus situation), 225-315 (power versus authority), 184-221, 319-79 (transactional versus transformational).

21. Douglas John Hall, *Thinking the Faith*, 158-69; *Professing the Faith: Christian Theology in a North American Context* (Minneapolis: Fortress Press, 1993), 286-95; *Confessing the Faith: Christian Theology in a North American Context* (Minneapolis: Fortress Press, 1996), 463-69.

22. Bruce C. Birch, "The Books of First and Second Samuel," *The New Interpreter's Bible, Volume II*, ed. Leander E. Keck, et al. (Nashville: Abingdon Press, 1998), 1002.

23. Ibid., 956-57, 1003, 1030-31, 1208-10, 1269, 1306-7, 1371-72, 1376-77.

24. Ibid., 957, 962, 1013-14, 1064-65, 1100, 1238-39, 1259-60.

25. Ibid., 957-58, 1072-73, 1128-29, 1136-37, 1171, 1198, 1203, 1252, 1294-95, 1326-27, 1340-42, 1359-60.

26. "Every procedure known to social science in general" has been applied to the study of leadership. That means that in addition to tests, questionnaires, and other forms of collecting data, the study of leadership also employs methods that are based more on narrative material: "autobiographical analysis; biographical analysis; case studies; the evaluation of news records, memoranda, and minutes of meetings; the analysis of speeches; . . . autologs and observers' logs of leaders' activities; . . . and individual interviews." Bernard M. Bass, *Handbook of Leadership*, 54-55.

27. Birch, "Samuel," 958-59, 983, 994-95, 1020-21, 1050, 1056-57, 1114, 1189, 1232.

28. Ibid., 959, 1007-8, 1082, 1267.

2. Sheep Without a Shepherd

1. Donald A. McGavran, *Understanding Church Growth*, 3rd edition, revised and edited by C. Peter Wagner (Grand Rapids, Mich.: William B. Eerdmans, 1990), 71-72.

2. Ronald A. Heifetz, *Leadership Without Easy Answers* (Cambridge, Mass.: Belknap Press of Harvard University Press, 1994), 36-40, 163-65, 260-62. For a church leadership practice that models Heifetz's emphasis on addressing adaptive issues see "the minimum factor," in Christian A. Schwarz, *Natural Church Development*, trans. Lynn McAdam, Lois Wollin, Martin Wollin (British Columbia, Canada: International Centre for Leadership Development and Evangelism, 1996), 49-60.

3. Norman Shawchuck, *Marketing for Congregations: Choosing to Serve People More Effectively* (Nashville: Abingdon Press, 1992), 57-64.

4. Douglas John Hall, *Thinking the Faith* (Minneapolis: Augsburg Press, 1989; Fortress Press edition, 1991), 200-7; *The End of Christendom and the Future of Christianity*, Christian Mission and Modern Culture (Harrisburg, Pa.: Trinity Press International, 1995), 1-18; Darrell L. Guder, ed., *Missional Church: A Vision for the Sending of the Church in North America* (Grand Rapids, Mich.: William B. Eerdmans, 1998), chap. 3.

5. Kelley's thesis is that churches with "traits of strictness" like Jehovah's Witnesses, Seventh-day Adventists, and the Mormons are growing because their members have a greater intensity of belief and level of commitment. (1) They put more time and effort into their cause. (2) They have a stronger conviction of being right. (3) They are linked more closely for mutual support. (4) They subordinate personal desires and ambitions to the shared goals of the group. Dean M. Kelley, *Why Conservative Churches Are Growing: A Study in Sociology of Religion* (New York: Harper & Row, 1972; Macon, Ga.: Mercer University Press, Rose Edition reprint, 1986), 51, 78.

6. Ibid., xix-xxi.

7. A certain iconoclastic attitude toward church leadership seems the norm for churches in America, but there are important exceptions such as pastors in African American denominations, pastors in first and second generation Korean churches, and pastors in the

recent "mega" churches. Eventually leadership in these venues also will be tempered by the climate of the volunteer nature of the church in America; but the point is that alternative narratives of respect for the office of the pastor exist: African tribal priest, Confucian scholar elder, heroic entrepreneur. They are worth holding up against the present practices of disrespect in the mainstream Protestant church, practices often lacking any narrative justification.

8. Nathan O. Hatch, *The Democratization of American Christianity* (New Haven and London: Yale University Press, 1989), chap. 8.

9. There is intriguing and overwhelming evidence to support the universal need for and practice of leadership. The evidence comes from history with its stories of the strategic difference made by military or political leaders. It comes from zoology with its phenomenon of dominance in primates. It comes from anthropology where there is no society without some leadership differentiation. It comes from studies of group dynamics where even informal groups tend to select and authorize one of their members to lead. It even comes from the study of children with their tendency to generate systems of stratification. Bernard M. Bass, *Handbook of Leadership*, 8-10; Heifetz, *Leadership Without Easy Answers*, chap. 3.

10. The Protestant protest against the Roman Catholic view of ordination as a sacrament was never intended to demean the conferral of grace for the function of the office of the pastor. See Wolfhart Pannenberg, *Systematic Theology, Volume 3*, trans. Geoffrey W. Bromiley (Grand Rapids, Mich.: William B. Eerdmans; Edinburgh: T & T Clark, 1998), 397-99. A church that can no longer remember the substance of its theology of ordination is hard-pressed to defend some of its practices such as holding to the unrepeatable nature of ordination or drawing a distinction between leave of absence and defrocking of clergy. For a sobering contemporary example of such theological alienation see Letty M. Russell's expressed regret over her Presbyterian ordination. *Church in the Round: Feminist Interpretation of the Church* (Louisville: Westminster John Knox Press, 1993), 53.

11. Bass, *Handbook of Leadership*, 7-8, 38-42, 579-86.

12. There are serious issues of corporate receptivity such as the level of impersonal bureaucratic resistance, the availability of mentoring

relationships, and the possibility of integrating individual and organizational goals. But there are also some nonnegotiable areas of personal competence such as management of attention, management of meaning, management of trust, and management of self. Warren Bennis, *Why Leaders Can't Lead: The Unconscious Conspiracy Continues* (San Francisco: Jossey-Bass, 1989), 19-24.

13. Michael Welker calls attention to the "early and unclear experiences of the Spirit" in the books of Samuel where the calling of a leader is accompanied by (but not necessarily the causal agent for) a dramatic change in readiness of persons for solidarity and collective action. Michael Welker, *God the Spirit*, trans. John F. Hoffmeyer (Minneapolis: Fortress Press, 1994), chap. 2. There are similar expressions of this simultaneous divine intervention for the sake of timely leadership throughout 1 and 2 Samuel.

3. Called

1. Four of the most widely used assessment tools for candidates for ministry are (1) the Minnesota Multiphasic Personality Inventory II (MMPII) that helps candidates discover personal strengths and areas of needed growth; (2) the Incomplete Sentences test that helps candidates name feelings about self, family, authority, and social awareness; (3) the Adjective Check List (ACL) that helps candidates assess self and relationship awareness; and (4) the Strong-Campbell Interest Inventory (SCII) that helps candidates understand their work preferences. There are debates among the gatekeepers that lead to the choice of these or other assessment tools. The language of biblical theology is often underrepresented in or absent from these debates.

2. For a survey of contemporary instruments see, "Assessment and Forecasting of Leaders' and Managers' Performance" in Bernard M. Bass, *Handbook of Leadership*, 857-78.

3. Birch, "Samuel," 1040-41.

4. The very proper Anglican John Wesley (1703–1791) was adamantly opposed to outdoor preaching at the start of his ministry. Convicted by his own theological development to find ways to express the gospel in indigenous forms and inspired by the example

of the Presbyterian revivalist George Whitefield, Wesley eventually submitted to his call to "be more vile." Richard P. Heitzenrater, *Wesley and the People Called Methodists* (Nashville: Abingdon Press, 1995), 98-103.

5. Human openness in contrast to biological fate or animal instinct is a fascinating datum of anthropology. It can be discussed in solely secular terms, but it also can be linked to such theological themes as humans created in the image of God, providence, and the coming reign of God. If God is the power of the future that matters then God is the final source of new possibilities for persons, societies, and creation. See Wolfhart Pannenberg's lifelong project of interpreting the anthropological datum of human openness in *What Is Man? Contemporary Anthropology in Theological Perspective*, trans. Duane A. Priebe (Philadelphia: Fortress Press, 1970), 1-13; *Anthropology in Theological Perspective*, trans. Matthew J. O'Connell (Philadelphia: Westminster Press, 1985), 43-79; *Systematic Theology, Volume 2*, trans. Geoffrey W. Bromiley (Grand Rapids, Mich.: William B. Eerdmans, 1994), 228-30.

6. For a study of the dissonance between the self-image of gatekeepers and their performance as it relates to acquaintance with the biblical call language, see Thomas K. Cartwright, "Creating a Culture of the Call in the Central Pennsylvania Conference of The United Methodist Church" (D.Min. project paper, Wesley Theological Seminary, 2003), 75-76, 83-84.

7. Generation X persons answering the call to ministry in mainline churches talk about growing up in a church where they had few friends their own age. They engage in a discernment process where their lack of experience is too often considered a detriment. They anticipate pastoring churches where they will be younger than the average age of the parishioner in the pew. See N. J. A. Humphrey, *Gathering the Next Generation: Essays on the Formation and Ministry of GenX Priests* (Harrisburg, Penn.: Morehouse Publishing, 2000).

8. In secular leadership studies Ronald Heifetz has developed the theme of the need to "Protect Voices of Leadership from Below," a theme that has special relevance to the work of gatekeepers. See Heifetz, *Leadership Without Easy Answers*, 128, 144, 186, 207, 270-71; Ronald A. Heifetz and Donald L. Laurie, "The Work of Leadership," in *Harvard Business Review on Leadership*

(Boston: Harvard Business School Press, 1998), 171-77.

9. Birch, "Samuel," 1099-1100.

10. Ibid., 1041.

11. See "Education in the Future Tense" in Alvin Toffler, *Future Shock* (New York: Random House, 1970; Bantam Books edition, 1971), chap. 18.

12. On the significance of the irreversibility of the world process to the Christian doctrine of creation, see Wolfhart Pannenberg, *Toward a Theology of Nature: Essays on Science and Faith*, ed. Ted Peters (Louisville: Westminster John Knox Press, 1993), 86-96. For a translation of this doctrine into a theological ethics that opposes contemporary claims of self-realization in every direction ("the voluntaristic misunderstanding") see Trutz Rendtorff, *Ethics, Volume 1: Basic Elements and Methodology in an Ethical Theology*, trans. Keith Crim (Philadelphia: Fortress Press, 1986), 33-40.

4. Envy

1. Dante Alighieri, *The Divine Comedy Volume II: Purgatory*, Translation with introduction, notes, and commentary by Mark Musa (New York: Penguin Classics, 1985), Canto XIII, ll.70-72.

2. Ibid., Canto XIII, ll.110-11.

3. Ibid., 146-47.

4. From the sixth century, in *The Rule of Saint Benedict*, see the sections on "Private Ownership by Monks," "Clothing and Shoes," and "The Brothers Ought to Obey One Another." *The Rule of Saint Benedict*, translated with introduction and notes by Anthony C. Meisel and M. L. del Mastro (New York: Doubleday Image Books, 1975), 76, 91-92, 105. From the eighteenth century see the questions on salary, benefits, and "superfluity in dress" asked of early American Methodist preachers at annual conference. Robert Emory, *History of the Discipline of the Methodist Episcopal Church*, revised by W. P. Strickland (New York: Carlton and Porter, 1857), 11, 13, 14, 18, 21. From the twentieth century see the chapter on "Relationships with Other Ministers" in Nolan B. Harmon, *Ministerial Ethics and Etiquette*, 2nd revised edition (Nashville: Abingdon Press, 1987), chap. 4.

5. St. John Chrysostom, *Six Books on the Priesthood,* translated with an introduction by Graham Neville (Crestwood, N.Y.: St. Vladimir's Seminary Press, 1977), 77.

6. Richard Baxter, *The Reformed Pastor,* edited with an introduction by John T. Wilkinson (London: Epworth Press, 1939), 95.

7. Robert Schnase, *Ambition in Ministry: Our Spiritual Struggle with Success, Achievement, and Competition* (Nashville: Abingdon Press, 1993), chap. 3.

8. Joe E. Trull and James E. Carter, *Ministerial Ethics: Being a Good Minister in a Not-So-Good World* (N.p.: Broadman & Holman, 1993), 201-2, 222 (Methodist), 223 (Presbyterian), 224 (Unitarian), 227 (Disciples), 238 (United Church of Christ).

9. There are pockets of resistance in mainline churches and whole segments of the Church Universal where the biblical warrant for women in ordained pastoral leadership remains unproved or ignored. So there is the enduring need to revisit the biblical and theological arguments. But in most mainline churches today the pressing questions arise around practice. Is leadership an essentially gender neutral art? Should women lead as men lead or do they bring alternative gifts to leadership? Do those with the power to send or bring persons to responsible positions appreciate those alternative gifts? If women lead "in a different voice" what is the long-term impact of their leadership upon the churches they lead? See Judith Orr, "Administration as an Art of Shared Vision," in *The Arts of Ministry: Feminist-Womanist Approaches,* edited by Christie Cozad Neuger (Louisville: Westminster John Knox Press, 1996), chap. 5; and "The Web: What It Is and How It Feels," in Susan Willhauck and Jacqulyn Thorpe, *The Web of Women's Leadership: Recasting Congregational Ministry* (Nashville: Abingdon Press, 2001), chap. 1.

10. Birch, "Samuel," 1119.

11. Donald Capps, *Deadly Sins and Saving Virtues* (Philadelphia: Fortress Press, 1987), 39-45.

12. Henry Fairlie, *The Seven Deadly Sins Today,* with drawings by Vint Lawrence (Notre Dame: University of Notre Dame Press, 1978, paperback edition, 1979), 69-74.

13. John Rawls, *A Theory of Justice,* revised edition (Cambridge, Mass.: Harvard University Press, 1971; Belknap Press revised edition, 1999), 465-74.

14. According to Jeremy Taylor's pastoral care classic, *The Rule and Exercises of Holy Dying*, we fight the final battle with envy when we are forced into a position of withdrawal and passiveness, that is, we become sick unto dying. The remedy is repentance, and the repentance that is effective replaces envy with generosity. "An envious man, if he gives God hearty thanks for the advancement of his brother, hath done an act of mortification of his envy, as directly as corporal austerities are an act of chastity, and an enemy to uncleanness." *The Rule and Exercises of Holy Dying*, A New Edition (London: Rivingtons, 1880), 147. The image of being able to acknowledge each other's gifts, at last (!), is arresting.

15. How can ordained persons retain their sense of uniqueness in a climate where the ministry of all Christians is used to denigrate their set apart status? Why not a reform of the clergy salary system to level the discrepancies and give greater priority to mission in deployment? If a civil service model of hiring, measuring merit, and promoting is not to be used for clergy, what model is? Or is it possible that there is more than one applicable model for differentiating and awarding clergy? How can judicatory supervisors address inequities of the past without creating new inequities in the future? What would it take to reintroduce solidarity to clergy who have lost the feel for collegiality and have become comfortable in the persona of Lone Ranger?

16. Anyone who has been involved in tense exchanges or public debates over equity among church leaders knows how difficult it is for church leaders to talk about these issues. The tendency to fast forward is always present. Compare this evasiveness to a series of straightforward articles in a recent publication by the Harvard Business School: "From Affirmative Action to Affirming Diversity," "A Modest Manifesto for Shattering the Glass Ceiling," "Mommy-Track Backlash," "The Truth About Mentoring Minorities: *Race Matters*," "Two Women, Three Men on a Raft," "Is This the Right Time to Come Out?" *Harvard Business Review on Managing Diversity*, Harvard Business School Paperback Series (Boston: Harvard Business School Press, 2002).

17. Birch, "Samuel," 1126-27.

18. *The American Heritage Dictionary of the English Language*, 3rd edition (Boston: Houghton Mifflin Company, 1992).

19. This way of "telling time" clashes with the prevailing secular culture's measures of time, as pastoral leaders who hold out for the integrity of the church seasons of Advent or Lent will attest. This means that the church leader's stream of consciousness, narrative flavored with the sequence of sacred calendar, can itself become an intentional act of leadership. The church leader is always answering the question, "What time is it?" in a way that is more or less dissonant with the answer most persons would give to that question. See Laurence Hull Stookey, *Calendar: Christ's Time for the Church* (Nashville: Abingdon Press, 1996), 17-38.

20. The automatic movement from character to plot, a phenomenon amply identified by writers talking about their craft, should also encourage pastoral leaders who for one reason or another have lost the narrative feel of their work and or ministry context. Stories are there, waiting to come out. See Anne Lamott, *Bird by Bird: Some Instructions on Writing and Life* (New York: Pantheon Books, 1994; Anchor Books Edition, 1995), 54-63.

21. Thomas Edward Frank, *The Soul of the Congregation: An Invitation to Congregational Reflection* (Nashville: Abingdon Press, 2000), 36-56.

22. This description of the active manager comes from Henry Mintzberg, "The Manager's Job: Folklore and Fact." The description of the pragmatic manager comes from Nitin Nohria and James D. Berkley, "Whatever Happened to the Take-Charge Manager?" *Harvard Business Review on Leadership* (Boston: Harvard Business School Press, A Harvard Business Review Paperback, 1998), 1-36, 199-222.

23. Elie Wiesel, *Souls on Fire: Portraits and Legends of Hasidic Masters*, trans. Marion Wiesel (New York: Summit Books, 1972), 120.

5. Set Apart

1. In United Methodist Polity, for instance, all candidates for ordained ministry are required to agree that they are "willing to assume supervisory responsibilities within the connection." *The Book of Discipline of The United Methodist Church 2000* (Nashville:

The United Methodist Publishing House, 2000), (219/par. 331, 2e). This service "above and beyond" is bounded by term limits (282/par. 418) and/or a mandatory retirement age (272/par. 409.1).

2. The phrase "paradigm shift" is one of the most overused and misused phrases in contemporary church leadership literature. As introduced by Thomas S. Kuhn, *The Structure of Scientific Revolutions* (Chicago: University of Chicago Press, 1962; Phoenix Edition, 1964), 66-76, the concept has rich interpretive potential. The literature of church leadership still lacks a serious attempt to hold together its theology of creation and the practice of leadership. It offers no alternative to Margaret J. Wheatley's synthesis of natural science and leadership written from an eclectic religious perspective in *Leadership and the New Science: Discovering Order in a Chaotic World*, 2nd edition (San Francisco: Berrett-Kochler, 1999).

3. Arthur P. Boers, *Never Call Them Jerks: Healthy Responses to Difficult Behavior* (Bethesda, Md.: Alban Institute, 1992), chap. 7.

4. Bruce C. Birch, "The Books of First and Second Samuel," *The New Interpreter's Bible, Volume II* (Nashville: Abingdon Press, 1998), 1347.

5. Discipleship under an eschatological prophet can be contrasted with two other models of discipleship current in Jesus' setting. Unlike the analogy of a rabbi and his disciples: (1) discipleship does not occur in the stable environment of a house; (2) it is not undertaken as a temporary commitment ending in "graduation"; (3) it is not committed to a fixed tradition; and (4) it is not limited to men. Unlike the analogy of a Cynic philosopher and his disciples: (1) discipleship does not try to model self-sufficiency; (2) it has a much more rigorous asceticism; (3) it anticipates an imminent future fulfillment; and (4) it manifests an outpouring of charismatic gifts. The first characteristic of a disciple of Jesus the eschatological prophet is "self-stigmatization." Gerd Theissen and Annette Merz, *The Historical Jesus: A Comprehensive Guide*, trans. John Bowden (Minneapolis: Fortress Press, 1998), 213-17.

6. H. Richard Niebuhr and Daniel D. Williams, ed., *The Ministry in Historical Perspectives* (New York: Harper & Brothers, 1956), ix-x, 5, 17-18, 65-66, 92-95, 112, 194-96, 242-43, 256-58, 271-76.

7. It is the unfinished legacy of the historical mandates for the ministry of all Christians from Martin Luther, *The Babylonian*

Captivity of the Church (1520), to the Decree on the Apostolate of the Laity of Vatican II (1966). Some secular writers seem to have a better read on the unfinished agenda than do the theologians of the practice of ministry. See Robert K. Greenleaf, *Servant Leadership: A Journey into the Nature of Legitimate Power and Greatness* (New York/Mahwah: Paulist Press, 1977), 79-82; and Peter F. Drucker, *Managing the Non-Profit Organization: Principles and Practices* (New York: HarperCollins, 1990; HarperBusiness edition, 1992), 161-69.

8. For the interpretation of theology as an academic enterprise that is both true to its own object (God) yet sensitive to criteria of credibility used by secular sciences, see Wolfhart Pannenberg, *Theology and the Philosophy of Science*, trans. Francis McDonagh (Philadelphia: Westminster Press, 1976), 326-45. Theology's subject is God, the all-determining reality who can only be known with certainty at the end of time, when the kingdom of God is complete. Until then theology is limited to anticipations of the totality of meaning, anticipations that function like hypothesis in the natural sciences where reality is also described provisionally.

9. Edward L. Long, Jr., *Patterns of Polity: Varieties of Church Governance* (Cleveland: Pilgrim Press, 2001), 151-57.

10. See "Extending beyond the condition of being tied to a particular time and situation: What is meant by the 'pouring out of the Spirit from heaven?'" in Michael Welker, *God the Spirit*, trans. John F. Hoffmeyer (Minneapolis: Fortress Press, 1994), 134-47.

6. Ducking Spears

1. See "The Sovereign Audience," in Nathan O. Hatch, *The Democratization of American Christianity* (New Haven and London: Yale University Press, 1989), chap. 5.

2. Daniel Goleman, *Emotional Intelligence* (New York: Bantam Books, 1995; Bantam trade paperback edition, 1997), 13-29, 59-65; Daniel Goleman, *Working with Emotional Intelligence* (New York: Bantam Books, 1998; Bantam trade paperback edition, 2000), 73-83; Daniel Goleman, Richard Boyatzis, Annie McKee,

Primal Leadership: Realizing the Power of Emotional Intelligence (Boston: Harvard Business School Press, 2002), 80-83.

3. See the deadly sin of Ira in Henry Fairlie, *The Seven Deadly Sins Today, Drawings by Vint Lawrence* (Notre Dame: University of Notre Dame Press, 1978), 87-109; Donald Capps, *Deadly Sins and Saving Virtues* (Philadelphia: Fortress Press, 1987), 28-32; Solomon Schimmel, *The Seven Deadly Sins: Jewish, Christian, and Classical Reflections on Human Nature* (New York: Free Press, 1992), 83-110.

4. This is Howard Beale's famous line as Peter Finch in the prophetic movie satire of network television news, *Network*, prod. & direct. Sidney Lumet, script by Paddy Chayefsky, Warner Studios, 1976.

5. Church growth often short-changes clergy power by restricting it to the dimension of charismatic gifts of persuasion (Spirit endowment) and reflective practice. The absence of engagement with classical ecclesiology is apparent. The saving remnant perspective often errs in the other direction. By conveying an image of the church as stripped of its alleged former glory it often implies a generalized loss of status, and hence power, of church leaders. Further empirical search for the real power of church leaders is discouraged.

6. Thomas C. Oden, *Becoming a Minister*, Clinical Pastoral Care Series, Volume 1 (New York: Crossroad, 1987), 32-34.

7. Niebuhr and Williams, ed., *The Ministry in Historical Perspectives*; Messer, *Contemporary Images of Christian Ministry*.

8. The most apparent temptation associated with the power of holding an office that inspires public trust is the temptation to lead a double life. And there are new versions of Elmer Gantry every generation. But there is also the temptation to run from the existence of social projections and send out contradictory messages of identity. There are church leaders who live out the drama of being set apart but live in constant denial: "I'm no different than one of you; just call me Sally."

9. Earl E. Sharp and Ronald H. Sunderland, ed., *The Pastor as Theologian* (New York: Pilgrim Press, 1988), 11-29; Thomas C. Oden, *Pastoral Theology: Essentials of the Ministry* (Harper SanFrancisco, 1983), 141-52; Richard Robert Osmer, *A Teachable*

Spirit: Recovering the Teaching Office in the Church (Louisville: Westminster John Knox Press, 1990), 139-74; Christie Cozad Neuger ed., *The Arts of Ministry: Feminist-Womanist Approaches* (Louisville: Westminster John Knox Press, 1996), 60-87.

10. The reality of charismatic leadership as the simultaneous action of the Spirit on two fronts, the Spirit empowering the individual to lead and the Spirit empowering a people to respond, is a repeated theme in the early sections of the Hebrew Bible. See Michael Welker, *God the Spirit*, trans. John F. Hoffmeyer (Minneapolis: Fortress Press, 1994), chap. 2. Max Weber's classical work on charismatic leadership faithfully captured this sense of the simultaneous action of the Spirit. Many writers in secular leadership studies after Weber lose sight of the second movement and reduce leadership to the heroic traits of the individual alone. See "Charismatic, Charismalike, and Inspirational Leadership," in Bernard M. Bass, *Bass and Stogdill's Handbook of Leadership*, 3rd edition (New York: Free Press, 1990), chap. 12.

11. For the dangers of the charismatic style of leadership to both the leader and the congregation, see Edwin H. Friedman, *Generation to Generation: Family Process in Church and Synagogue* (New York: Guilford Press, 1989), 220-34.

12. Jackson W. Carroll, *As One with Authority: Reflective Leadership in Ministry* (Louisville, Ky.: Westminster John Knox Press, 1991), chap. 6. Carroll is applying to ministry the term "reflective practice" as borrowed from Donald A. Schön, *The Reflective Practitioner: How Professionals Think in Action* (New York: Basic Books, 1983).

7. Dancing Madly

1. Sirach 44:1 NRSV. The litany of great persons with their traits is given in Sirach 44:1–51:24.

2. *Plutarch's Lives, Volume 1*, trans. John Dryden, ed. and preface, Arthur Hugh Clough, intro. Jams Atlas (New York: Modern Library Paperback, 2001), e.g., 50, 102, 145, 256.

3. Niccolo Machiavelli, *The Prince*, 2nd edition, trans. and intro. Harvey C. Mansfield (Chicago: University of Chicago Press, 1998), chaps. 14–17.

4. Thomas Carlye, *On Heroes, Hero-worship, and the Heroic in History* (New York: M. M. Caldwell Co., 1840).

5. William James, *The Will to Believe and Other Essays in Popular Philosophy and Human Immortality: Two Supposed Objections to the Doctrine* (New York: Dover Publications, 1956), 216-54.

6. Bernard M. Bass, *Bass & Stogdill's Handbook of Leadership: Theory, Research, and Managerial Applications*, 3rd edition (New York: Free Press, 1990), 80-81, 192-95, 211.

7. Bass offers the following summation of half a century of studies on leadership traits. "The average person who occupied a position of leadership exceeded the average member of his or her group, to some degree," in ten areas: sociability, initiative, persistence, execution, self-confidence, intuition, collaboration, popularity, adaptability, and ability to articulate. *Handbook of Leadership,* 75.

8. Andrew S. Grove, *Only the Paranoid Survive: How to Exploit the Crisis Points That Challenge Every Company* (New York: Doubleday, A Currency Book, 1996; Currency Paperback Edition, 1999).

9. Edwin H. Friedman, *Generation to Generation: Family Process in Church and Synagogue* (New York: Guilford Press, 1985), 27. Those like Friedman who work in the family systems approach acknowledge their debt to Murray Bowen for his pioneering work in family therapy.

10. The "school" of emotional intelligence thought at a minimum includes three figures. David McClelland first questioned the correlation between IQ and leadership ability. Howard Gardner interjected the concept of "multiple intelligences" to the study of developmental psychology. And Daniel Goleman and colleagues continue to apply emotional intelligence to a variety of private and public venues. See Daniel Goleman, *Emotional Intelligence* (New York: Bantam Books, 1995; Bantam Trade Paperback, 1997), chap 3.

11. Daniel Goleman, Richard Boyatzis, and Annie McKee, *Primal Leadership: Realizing the Power of Emotional Intelligence* (Boston: Harvard Business School, 2002), chaps. 3–4.

12. Ronald A. Heifetz, *Leadership Without Easy Answers,* 252-63.

13. J. Clinton McCann, Jr., "The Book of Psalms: Introduction, Commentary, and Reflections," *The New Interpreter's Bible, Volume IV* (Nashville: Abingdon Press, 1996), 776-71.

14. I am combining two theological themes from Wolfhart Pannenberg. The first is his study of the phenomenon of primal trust, the "in what" do I find myself? experience that precedes all conscious choice and sets the foundation for healthy personality development, religious faith, and the reflective interpretation that precedes all action. Wolfhart Pannenberg, *Anthropology in Theological Perspective*, trans. Matthew J. O'Connell (Philadelphia: Westminster Press, 1985), 224-42. The second is his study of prayer that he places under the doctrine of love in his systematic theology. Prayer is ecstatic response in speech to experiences of the goodness of existence (thanksgiving), of the openness of the future (intercession), of remorse for wrong (confession), and of the assurance of God's final victory (praise). Prayer is the Spirit's gift of elevating persons to an intensified relationship with God. Wolfhart Pannenberg, *Systematic Theology, Volume 3*, trans. Geoffrey W. Bromiley (Grand Rapids, Mich.: William B. Eerdmans; Edinburgh: T & T Clark, 1998), 202-11. David embodies such primal trust and ecstatic speech.

15. Bernard Bass's exhaustive survey of this literature runs to more than 250 pages. A common theme is the inapplicability of past taxonomies of "manager" and "leader" to contemporary organizations with their complexity and rate of change. *Handbook of Leadership*, 383-559.

16. A favorite technique of some church growth literature, where "leaders" so obviously wear the white hats and "managers" (a.k.a., "chaplains" or "guardians of the status quo") wear the black hats.

17. See R. Alec MacKenzie's diagram, "Leadership and Management Elements, Tasks, Functions, and Activities" in Bass, *Handbook of Leadership*, 387.

18. Pastoral theologian Donald Capps frequently addresses the difference between guilt and shame and the particular difficulty Christians have differentiating. See especially, *The Depleted Self* (Minneapolis: Fortress Press, 1993); *Agents of Hope: A Pastoral*

Psychology (Minneapolis: Fortress Press, 1995); and *Jesus: A Psychological Biography* (St. Louis: Chalice Press, 2000).

19. Stephen Pattison, *Shame: Theory, Therapy, Theology* (London: Cambridge University Press, 2000), 3, 61-64.

20. Ibid., 71-78.

21. Shame inhibits forbidden drives and prepares individuals for life in society. It is an appeasement-related response that allows the offending individual to be restored to the group. It guards the boundaries of the self from total immersion in others. It reveals personal ideals and values and holds them up for scrutiny. Ibid., 78-82.

8. Infidelity

1. The Protestant clergy captured in the novels of John Updike and the Catholic priests captured in the novels of Mary Gordon resist neat psychological, moral, or political analysis. They are complex, reflective persons as well as agents of harm. The fullness of their stories, the genuineness of religious restlessness, the surrender of creative imagination to evil, the vision of redeemed children of God on the other side of sexual politics, all together offer a note of caution in the present climate of quick and decisive judgment. They also forecast the long work of unraveling that must occur before the minister who falls is ready to take up the call to church leadership once more.

2. See "The Mystic's Orgasm: Eros in the Spiritual Life" in Thomas Moore, *The Soul of Sex: Cultivating Life as an Act of Love* (New York: HarperCollins, 1998), chap. 7.

3. It is easy for those who supervise church leaders through errant episodes to forget the privileged position of the leader in those episodes in terms of access to the resources for restoration: a caring community, counseling, and the language for repentance and forgiveness. The growing edge for the church's response in this area is the sharing of those resources with the other party as well as the families of the leader. This is not (or should not be) a matter of shielding against litigation. It is a matter of restorative justice.

4. Homer, *The Odyssey*, Bk. 12. The realism behind this practice, its recognition of both the power of certain temptations and the strength for resistance in clergy connection, has fascinated writers

on church leadership from the fourth century to the present beginning with St. John Chrysostom, *Six Books on the Priesthood*, trans.
with intro. by Graham Neville (Crestwood, N.Y.: St. Vladimir's
Seminary, 1977), III. 7, p. 77

5. Charles Wesley's hymn "And Are We Yet Alive" (1749) captures the drama of itinerant ministry and the joy of the annual
incoming of the survivors.

> And are we yet alive, and see each other's face?
> Glory and thanks to Jesus give for his almighty grace!
>
> . . . .
>
> What troubles have we seen, what mighty conflicts past,
> Fightings without, and fears within, since we assembled last!
>
> . . . .
>
> Yet out of all the Lord hath brought us by his love;
> And still he doth his help afford, and hides our life above.

The United Methodist Hymnal (Nashville: The United Methodist
Publishing House, 1989), no. 553. Church leaders who are engaged
fully in the public drama of their church stories have a certain inoc-
ulation against some temptations. Withdrawal from the public
drama, however understandable, is often the signal of lowered resistance to those temptations.

6. Birch, "Samuel," 1288-90.

7. Marie M. Fortune, *Is Nothing Sacred?: When Sex Invades the
Pastoral Relationship* (San Francisco: Harper & Row, 1989). See
*Center for the Prevention of Sexual and Domestic Violence: An
Educational Resource on Abuse and Religion*, Web site available at
http://www.cpsdv.org/; accessed 20 September 2002.

8. John Keegan, *The Mask of Command* (New York: Viking
Penguin, 1987; Penguin Books, 1988), 286-310.

9. Ronald A. Heifetz and Marty Linsky analyze the affair of
President Bill Clinton and Monica Lewinsky in terms of the leader's
retreat from the political battlefield in *Leadership on the Line: Staying
Alive Through the Dangers of Leading* (Boston: Harvard Business
School Press, 2002), chap. 8.

10. Peter F. Drucker, *Management Challenges for the 21st Century*
(New York: HarperCollins, 1999; HarperBusiness paperback , 2001),

123-32; Edgar H. Schein, *Organizational Culture and Leadership, Second Edition* (San Francisco: Jossey-Bass Publishers, 1992; paperback edition, 1997), 298-99; Daniel Goleman, *Working with Emotional Intelligence* (New York: Bantam Books, 1998; paperback edition, 2000), chap. 7.

11. Sissela Bok, *Lying: Moral Choice in Public and Private Life* (New York: Random House, 1978; Vintage Books edition, 1979), 14, 26-28, 69.

12. For the interpretation of temptation as a lure from one's true story see Stanley Hauerwas, *The Peaceable Kingdom: A Primer in Christian Ethics* (New York: Harcourt, Brace, and Company, 1956), 121-30.

13. Thomas C. Oden, *Classical Pastoral Care, Volume 3: Pastoral Counsel* (Grand Rapids, Mich.: Baker Books, 1987), chap. 6.

14. Ibid., 172-76.

15. *The Book of Discipline of The United Methodist Church 2000* (Nashville: The United Methodist Publishing House, 2000), par. 164 b, 2701.9; 2707; *The Doctrine and Discipline of the African Methodist Episcopal Church 2000–2004* (Nashville: AMEC Publishing House, 2001), pt. XI, sec. 1, 325-326; *The Constitution of the Presbyterian Church (U.S.A.), Part II: Book of Order 2000–2001* (Louisville: The Office of the General Assembly, 2000), D-1.0101 – D-1.0103; John P. Beal, James A. Coriden, and Thomas J. Green, ed., *New Commentary on the Code of Canon Law* (New York: Paulist Press, 2000), 1492 on Canon 1288; Charles W. Deweese, *Baptist Church Covenants* (Nashville: Broadman Press, 1990), 209-10.

9. Private Tears, Public Faces

1. Peter M. Senge, *The Fifth Discipline: The Art & Practice of The Learning Organization* (New York: Currency Doubleday, 1990; Currency paperback edition, 1994), 306-12.

2. Ibid., 312.

3. Bonnie J. Miller-McLemore, *Also a Mother: Work and Family as Theological Dilemma* (Nashville: Abingdon Press, 1994), 75, 112-13, 180.

4. "It is probably the case that a highly integrated person has an implicit, if not consciously affirmed, order of loves. Some objects

have primacy; perhaps a single object or end is primary. Other loves are ordered in relation to the primary object, and human activities are shaped and graded in importance by the ordering of loves; the ordering of valuations." James M. Gustafson, *Ethics from a Theocentric Perspective, Volume 1: Theology and Ethics* (Chicago: University of Chicago Press, 1981; paperback edition, 1983), 298. Gustafson is unfolding the implications of Kierkegaard's distinction between the divine and human. "We are to be absolutely related to the absolute and relatively related to the relative" (311).

5. Frederick Buechner, *Peculiar Treasures: A Biblical Who's Who* (San Francisco: Harper & Row, 1979).

6. William H. Willimon, *Calling and Character: Virtues of the Ordained Life* (Nashville: Abingdon Press, 2000), 27-28.

7. Martin Luther's marriage to Katharine von Boren in 1525 opened the floodgates of polemical debate on clerical marriage. It was a direct assault on the official Catholic position of clerical celibacy in force since the time of Gregory VII in the eleventh century. The debate capitalized on the new media of print and became quite animated, at times even coarse, over the next two decades.

It was an issue of doctrine that could be related to almost every controversy of the Reformation. Leading figures of the Reformation on the continent and in England weighed in: Luther (the commentary on 1 Corinthians 7, *The Antichrist, Table Talk*), Melanchthon (*A very godly defense . . . defending the marriage of priestes*), Bucer (*Gratultio*), Tyndale (*Anwser to Sir Thomas More's Dialogue*), Bale (*The Actes of the Englysh Votares*), Foxe (*Actes and Monuments*) and others. Traces of the debate live on in the Anglican Articles of Religion that are a doctrinal staple of the churches of the Methodist heritage.

The debate on clerical marriage eventually refocused from a critique of clerical celibacy to an assessment of the positive values of marriage. The vision was, in the words of the English legislation lifting the prohibition on clerical marriage, that clergy "might better attend to the ministration of the gospel, and be less intricated and troubled with the charge of household." Helen L. Parish, *Clerical Marriage and the English Reformation: Precedent, Policy and Practice* (Aldershot, England: Ashgate, 2000), 8-26, 180-91.

8. John Wall and Bonnie Miller-McLemore, "Health, Christian

Marriage Traditions, and the Ethics of Marital Therapy," in *Marriage, Health, and the Professions: If Marriage Is Good for You, What Does This Mean for Law, Medicine, Ministry, Therapy, and Business?* ed. John Wall et al. (Grand Rapids, Mich.: William B. Eerdmans, 2002), 186-207.

9. Robert D. Putnam, *Bowling Alone: The Collapse and Revival of American Community* (New York: Simon & Schuster, 2000; Touchstone edition, 2001). Putnam traces the universal impact of the loss of a culture of civic mindedness across a wide spectrum of service organizations from Scouts to PTAs. To the list of casualties add this: the parsonage family as a school for public service where civic virtues are taught and the call to a career in public service is often heard.

10. Leading from Providence

1. William Cowper, "God Moves in a Mysterious Way," 1774; *Olney Hymns* (London: W. Oliver, 1779).

2. Henry Mintzberg, "The Manager's Job: Folklore and Fact," in *Harvard Business Review on Leadership* (Harvard Business School Press, 1998), 1-36.

3. In secular leadership literature there are those who protest the quantification of leadership and the overly analytical accounts of what leaders do. See, for example, Henry Mintzberg, *The Nature of Managerial Work* (New York: Harper & Row, 1973); Max DePree, *Leadership Is an Art* (New York: Dell Publishing, 1989); and Lee Bolman and Terrance Deal, *Reframing Organizations: Artistry, Choice, Leadership* (San Francisco: Jossey-Bass, 1991).

4. Daniel J. Levinson, et al., *The Seasons of a Man's Life* (New York: Alfred A. Knopf, 1978), 91-92. Levinson outlines a scenario of healthy adult development around the concept of the life dream. "Those who betray the Dream in their twenties will have to deal later with the consequences. Those who build a life structure around the Dream in early adulthood have a better chance for present fulfillment, though years of struggle may be required to maintain the commitment and work toward its realization.

During the Mid-life Transition they will have to reappraise the magical aspects of the Dream and modify its place in their middle adult lives" (92). For a gender sensitive revision of Levinson's analysis, see Bonnie J. Miller-McLemore, *Also a Mother: Work and Family as Theological Dilemma* (Nashville: Abingdon Press, 1994), 41-63. The theological foundation for locating the lifelong search for identity in the context of God's providence is the interpretation of meaning as the relation of the parts to an unfinished but anticipated whole. This interpretation arose in the emancipation of the human sciences from the natural sciences and is associated with the name of Wilhem Dilthey. See Wolfhart Pannenberg, *Theology and the Philosophy of Science*, trans. Francis McDonagh (Philadelphia: Westminster Press, 1976), 72-80, 135-55, 206-24.

5. James M. Gustafson, *Ethics from a Theocentric Perspective, Volume 1: Theology and Ethics* (Chicago: University of Chicago Press, 1981; paperback edition, 1983), 264. Gustafson packs most of the elements of his theocentric vision of providence under the five phrases of this quote. If a person surrendered to this theocentric vision of providence a conspicuous shift in the character of relevant leadership posture would occur. Leadership would have to become more about learning than doing, more about adapting than controlling.

6. Terms like "middle knowledge" and "counterfactuals" originated in the theology of providence of the Spanish Jesuit, Luis de Molina (1535). The Molinist account of providence contrasts with the traditional interpretation of providence over the tightness of the connection between what God knows and wills and what is. For the Molinist God's foreknowledge always encompasses alternative realities, and God's involvement in creation and history are much more a continuous action and reaction than a foreordained planning. Alternative futures may depend on human initiative. Two Christmastime classics convey the Molinist contribution to a theology of providence. In Charles Dickens's *A Christmas Carol* (1843) The Ghost of Christmas Yet to Come points Scrooge to the shadows of things that *may be* but not *must* be. Charles Dickens, *A Christmas Carol* (Roslyn, N.Y.: Walter J. Black, 1965), Stave 5, 88. In Frank Capra's film, *It's a Wonderful Life* (1945), George Bailey is given the rare privilege of seeing how things would have been if he had never

been born. Thomas P. Flint, *Divine Providence: the Molinist Account,* Cornell Studies in the Philosophy of Religion, William P. Alston, ed. (Ithaca and London: Cornell University Press, 1998), 76-81. First and Second Samuel also summons church leaders to a drama where "the shadows of things that would have been may be dispelled."

7. The Stoic Epictetus provides a typically Stoic image of providence as predestination in this image. "Remember that you are an actor in a play, which is as the playwright wants it to be: short if he wants it short, long if he wants it long. If he wants you to play a beggar, play even this part skillfully, or a cripple, or a public official, or a public citizen. What is yours is to play the assigned part well. But to choose it belongs to someone else." Quoted in Flint, *Divine Providence,* 19.

8. Along with the crucial questions, "who is my Abigail?" (chapter 6) and "who is my Nathan?" (chapter 8), it is also helpful for the church leader to ask, who is my Eli? Who can prevent me from foreclosing on future options? Who mediates to me the challenge of a providential God to my tendency to reduce choices to either/or? Who can keep the "perhaps" in my grammar of faith?

9. Birch, "Samuel," 958.

10. Church leaders can grow in a spirituality of providence, and progress can be measured. In a nineteenth-century classic of spirituality, Jean-Pierre de Caussade offers possible indicators. To grow in abandonment to divine providence is to grow in "active loyalty" to God's work in creation (25) and to become more centered in one's own story (49). It means exchanging idealized projections of the past for an appreciation of God's activity in the present moment (50). It summons less dependence on social recognition (60). The overarching virtue is to become available to God's unfolding purposes in spite of obstacles. "It is a state of charmed delight in which the soul sleeps peacefully in the bosom of providence, plays innocently with the divine wisdom (Prov. 8:30), and feels no anxiety about the voyage which continues on its even, happy way in spite of rocks and pirates and continual storms" (69). Jean-Pierre de Caussade, *Abandonment to Divine Providence,* trans. and introduction by John Beevers (New York: Doubleday, Image Books, 1975).

11. In their bravado church growth advocates sometimes seem oblivious to this important theological distinction. "More church!" is not the point of providence. "It is God's design to gather all creation under the Lordship of Christ (Eph. 1:10), and to bring humanity and all creation into communion. As a reflection of the communion of the Triune God, the Church is called by God to be the instrument in fulfilling this goal. . . . As such it is not an end in itself, but a gift given the world in order that all may believe (John 17:21)." *The Nature and Purpose of the Church: A Sign on the Way to a Common Statement,* Faith and Order, Paper No. 181 (Switzerland: WCC/Faith and Order, 1998), 15.

12. Jonathan Edwards represents one end of the spectrum of approaches to congregational renewal in *The Faithful Narrative of the Surprising Work of God in the Conversion of Many Hundred Souls in Northampton* (1737). It is a posture of waiting with knowledge that renewal can happen but with no particular expectation that it will happen here and now. Charles Finney in *Lectures on Revivals of Religion* (1835) represents the other end of that spectrum. Renewal in congregations is a matter of choice and technique. Finney foreshadows church growth literature. Is there an approach between these two extremes, one where the church waits for the Spirit to move but positions itself to receive the blessing and cooperate with the action when the Spirit does move? For an analysis of these two extremes and the suggestion of a middle way, see Peter Mason Moon, "Shall We Gather at the River? Searching for the Seeds of God's Revival of Contemporary Methodism" (D.Min. project paper, Wesley Theological Seminary, 1999).

13. John Wesley's "Covenant Service," *The United Methodist Hymnal* (Nashville: The United Methodist Publishing House, 1989), no. 607.